EAST *of the* ROCKIES

The **LES MORGAN** *Story*

JEANNETTE MORGAN YIM
and **LES MORGAN**

Diane,
Hope you enjoy
my story!

Les

ISBN 13: 978-1-59152-198-3
Published by Jeannette Morgan Yim and Les Morgan
© 2017 by Jeannette Morgan Yim and Les Morgan

For more information, contact: yimjeannette@gmail.com

You may order extra copies of this book by calling
Farcountry Press toll free at (800) 821-3874.

sweetgrassbooks
an imprint of Farcountry Press
Produced by Sweetgrass Books.
PO Box 5630, Helena, MT 59604;
(800) 821-3874; www.sweetgrassbooks.com.

 Produced in the United States of America.

21   20   19   18   17   1   2   3   4   5

DEDICATION

This book is dedicated to the families of
Les Morgan and Jeannette Morgan Yim.

It is with hope that this book will be preserved and read
by the children, grandchildren, and great-grandchildren as
well as future generations of Roland and Georgiana Morgan.

This story takes place in the beautiful
Big Sky Country of Montana.

FAMILY MAP

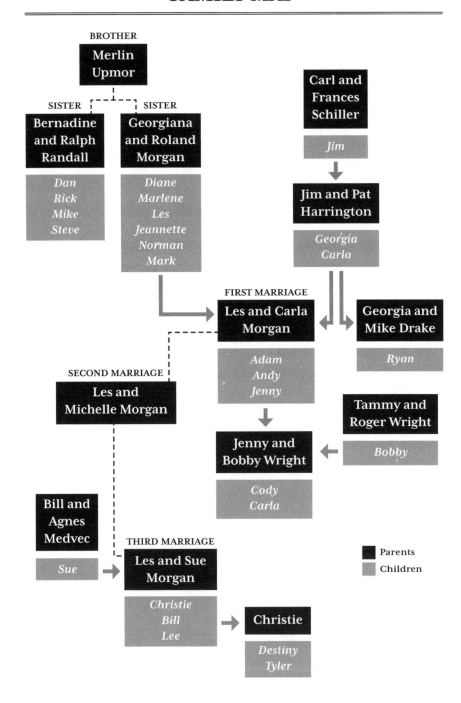

TABLE OF CONTENTS

PROLOGUE

Many people have asked me why I chose to write a book about my brother Les. My first response is why not? He is one of the people I most admire in this world. It appears that no matter what adversity has been set before him, he handles everything with such grace, strength, and dignity.

You can never quantify or explain a person's life on a few sheets of paper. What I am hoping to achieve is to give the reader (particularly his family) a sense of my brother Les. Who is this quiet man behind the struggles and triumphs of his life?

His story deserves to be told. And who better than Les to convey his story, telling it to me, his sister Jeannette, who has been with him since childhood. And so, the book is really a conversation between siblings, taking place during the years 2011 through 2015. Most of the information in this memoir is directly from Les with a few interjections and thoughts (in *italics*) from me.

This is a journey that we agreed to take together; I look forward to the challenge of it, and to the laughter and the tears that may come.

THE EARLY YEARS

This story about my brother, Les Morgan, takes place in Helena, Montana. Helena is the beautiful capital of Montana. It sits east of the Continental Divide in the Rocky Mountains and is surrounded by the Elkhorn Mountains to the south and the Big Belt Mountains to the north.

Les is the third child of six born to Roland and Georgiana Morgan. For the sake of clarification, he has two older sisters, Diane and Marlene; one younger sister, Jeannette (me); and two younger brothers, Norm and Mark. The family may have been complete when Les was born if it were not for the beliefs of my strong Catholic mother. I believe my Baptist-raised father felt that when the family grew to include three girls and three boys that was enough of a blessing.

This is a memoir—Les' life in his own words as told to me.

CHAPTER ONE

THE BEGINNING

It was snowing the day Mom brought me home from St. Johns Hospital in Helena, Montana. It was July 10, 1951. I remember Mom saying that she couldn't believe that she was bringing home a newborn baby in the middle of summer and it was snowing. This was the year that Montana forgot to have a summer.

It's difficult to know where to begin my story so I think I should start from my earliest memory, which was I believe around the age of two years. I remember Diane came home from school in a taxi-cab because she fell off a swing and was bleeding from the head; I think she needed stitches.

I have many early memories of events that occurred between the ages of four to five years old. I recall that even before I started school, I was great friends with my cousins Rick and Mike Randall; we alternately spent time at each other's houses. I think I was spending time at the Randall's house during the week because Uncle Ralph would stop on his way home from lunch every day and he would pick me up at my house. I think we were still living in the basement apartment at that time. Anyway, he picked me up in this great, big-ass truck (a freight hauling truck that he used while working for the Northern Pacific Railroad) and I thought it was so cool because I sat up really high. I played with my cousins and we spent the afternoon running around chasing each other inside and outside of the house. That's when the Randalls lived on the 1800 block of Hauser Boulevard. At that time it was a little bitty house that had been converted from a barn into a house. It was outside the city limits; the family had city water but their sewer was connected to some type of cesspool next to the house.

Once in a while I spent the night with Uncle Ralph and Aunt Bernadine, probably after nagging Mom to let me stay. I remember one morning—maybe a Saturday—I woke up and Uncle Ralph and Aunt Bernadine asked me if I remembered getting up and packing a box during the middle of the night. Of course I didn't remember because I was sleepwalking and I guess that I thought I was at my house. I remember being gently teased about packing boxes in the middle of the night! Another time I remember getting into trouble with Aunt Bernadine because Mike and I got into her closet and were playing with her Kotex. We took them out of the box and played with them like they were toys—we thought they were kind of neat and fun to play with. Aunt Bernadine sweetly said, "You boys get outta there, put those things back!" I believe we were only about four or five years old.

There was another time that Uncle Ralph came over in his big truck. He had picked up a load of goods that had come from Seattle. He showed us a huge wharf rat that he had found in the back of his truck. Uncle Ralph laid out the rat (the size of a large cat) and showed all of us. Over fifty years later I still remember that rat.

Uncle Ralph also worked for Eddy's Bakery (in Helena), where he learned to bake really great breads and everything. I remember going into the bakery with Mike and Rick. Uncle Ralph gave us a great tour. He showed us huge vats of bread dough and took us all over the bakery. There were all kinds of people working there and they were all nice to us. I remember the smells of dough rising; most likely we got some treats to eat.

Another significant memory I have of Uncle Ralph occurred before I started going to school (maybe around five or six years old). The Randalls had a cat, surprising now, because I never remembered the Randalls with a cat! Mike, Rick, and I went with Uncle Ralph to take their cat to the vet. Dr. Jasmine spayed the cat right in front of us—it really surprised me. I had to turn away when I saw the guts of the cat and passed out—the first time ever. I guess Uncle Ralph didn't see any problem with his kids and me watching a cat being spayed when we were all just little kids.

Yeah, I know Uncle Ralph was tough—he expected all of us to be tough. You were never "babied," even as a five-year-old.

CHAPTER TWO

MY MEMORIES OF UNCLE RALPH

*U*ncle Ralph was such a huge part of your childhood Les, "looming large" as they say; I think we need to discuss him. There is no way to sum up a person's life in a paragraph; however, there are some words that help describe him: Italian, poor, rough-tough childhood running free on the streets of Sacramento. He was smart, hardworking, a great cook, emotional, short fused, extremely passionate about politics, talked often about Jesus suffering on the cross, which would bring him to tears, was caring, and quick with the jokes: "Did you hear the one about . . . ?"

There was toughness in him that was like a strong twine weaving through his life. He was a 1st Special Service Force paratrooper, a soldier. He experienced pain from Hitler's army. The exploding shells in his back, leaving deep gouges along both sides of his spine. Many months spent in a military hospital, forget the pain: think about the pretty nurses, the nice docs. Remember Bernadine, never forget Bernadine, get up and walk out of this hospital and go back and marry sweet Bernadine. He was a prolific painter, painting with his right hand, and then painting with his left hand—mountain scenes, animals, trains, oceans, and the Oregon coast—he loved the Pacific. He was always suffering back pain, cigarettes and drinking did not help, pills did not help. He rode motorcycles, huge motorcycles bigger than Uncle Ralph himself. Suzukis: 350, 450, 550, 650, 750, always buying the next biggest 50. Ralph flew on top of the gigantic cycles, engines roaring—to the top of McDonald Pass and down as fast as his motorcycle could go—hard wind on his face and body, pushing him back against the bike, cigarette flying out of his mouth, forgetting the pain of childhood, the war, and the

death of his first-born son. Just Uncle Ralph and the wind and speed. Free
for a brief moment from emotional and physical pain. Ralph W. Randall,
husband, proud father of four sons, decorated WWII veteran. Hero.

I have a sweet, rare memory of Uncle Ralph. One time I was sitting in
the Randalls' living room in one of the big Lazy Boy reclining chairs next
to the kitchen. Uncle Ralph was sitting at the kitchen table; his elbow was
on the table with his chin resting on his hand. I don't know where everyone
else was—it was just me and Uncle Ralph. I think I was sixteen or seventeen
years old. I was explaining to Uncle Ralph the virtues of rock music and how
great the Beatles were. I remember thinking that they were the greatest band
to ever live. Uncle Ralph leaned toward me and said in a soft (but gravelly)
voice, "Jeannette, they don't write 'em like they used to." Suddenly he started
singing this song:

"As Time Goes By"
By Herman Hupfeld, 1931

"You must remember this,
a kiss is still a kiss,
a sigh is just a sigh;
the fundamental things apply,
as time goes by

and when two lovers woo,
they still say "I love you,"
on that you can rely;
no matter what the future brings,
as time goes by

Moonlight and love-songs never out of date,
hearts full of passion,
jealousy and hate;
woman needs man
and man must have his mate,

that no one can deny.
It's still the same old story,
a fight for love and glory, a case of do or die!
the world will always welcome lovers,
as time goes by."

As he was singing I stood up and walked over to Uncle Ralph and he kept singing. He sang the entire song—his pitch was perfect. When he finished the song he smiled, and I just stood there for a minute and thought I had never heard such a beautiful song in my entire life. I love looking back and finding the sweet memories.

CHAPTER THREE

MORE CHILDHOOD MEMORIES FROM LES

L es, I remember you mentioning a boy you used to play with a lot as a kid who you had some great adventures with; tell me more about this time in your life.

Well Jeannette, recently I was talking to my childhood friend Stefan and he reminded me of when we went into the empty house that Dad and I were building—I was Dad's helper.

Les! That is an understatement—but we can talk more about that later.

Stefan and I were swearing at the top of our lungs in the empty house, using every swear word we could think of; I think I was in sixth or seventh grade I suppose.

Les, it sounds like the two of you were having a great time! Something you could never have done in Catholic school—at least not say the words out loud! Who knows what the nuns would have done.

That's for sure! Another time Stefan and I were hiking to the top of Mount Helena, the sheer rock side of the mountain, and we went straight up and down the rocks instead of going around the mountain. Apparently there was a time when I was frozen in fear and Stefan had to help me get down from the top of the mountain. Stefan and I would take off on treks around the mountains behind Mount Helena. Some areas were really remote, especially for little kids. I remember finding Hale Reservoir back in the mountains and Stefan and I took off all of our clothes and we thought it was the greatest thing—I thought it was a swimming pool! I was nine or ten years old and we had spent the day hiking all over the hills.

We swam in Hale Reservoir before we moved into the new house on Hauser Boulevard that I helped Dad build. The house took seven years to build and it was still really rough when we moved in, probably in 1965 or 1966. I was in high school, probably a freshman before it was nearly done.

I remember moving into the new two-story red brick house, Les. It was Dad's dream. When we moved into it we had one finished bathroom (for eight people), stove, refrigerator, no cupboards, no carpet or linoleum, and bare wood floors. Bedrooms and closets were not finished. What the house did have was a lot more room, and a great big, beautiful stone fireplace in the family room downstairs that made up for some of its lack of creature comforts. I remember how hard you worked with Dad to build and finish that house. It took up many hours, days, weeks, months, and years of your childhood. What a good son you were.

Do you remember the red wagon? We got it for Christmas, the same year that you girls got the green bike—it was when I still believed in Santa Claus, around the age of six or seven. I think maybe Mom and Dad came into a little money that year, we had a good Christmas. I remember we were all shoved into one bedroom in the northwest corner of the house. We were all looking out of the window and saw flying red lights. Then, Santa came to the door and he walked loudly up the stairs, opened the door at the top of the stairs, and said, "HO, HO, HO, Merry Christmas!" And we all looked out of the window again and saw the flying red lights take off! I still don't know how Dad did that. Somehow Dad worked out the details and he made it absolutely convincing. We saw his sleigh come and go, and we were absolutely convinced that we saw Santa Claus and he came into our house and up our stairs! I was a believer. I think that was a Christmas around 1955 to 1957. That was a great Christmas.

Yes, I remember.

We had that wagon for a long, long time, and all of us would take it down the street and down the lot as fast as it would go. I remember a magpie parallel to the wagon right at our face level as we flew down the lot and it flew with us over and over again. The magpie was playing with us.

Also, when we were kids growing up in that house, two or three times Dad brought home injured birds, usually pigeons, and nurtured them back to health. Bringing a bird home was a dangerous prospect for that bird because we also had several cats and, gee, those cats were always trying to get in the bird's box to eat them. I think the birds were probably from East Helena, and the noxious gas from the American Smelting and Refining Company (ASARCO) was probably killing them. Years later, I was driving with Dad and he saw a bird that had been hit, maybe by a car. It was flopping around on the ground. We were driving down Grant Avenue, going toward Euclid Avenue, and we stopped the car and walked over to the bird. So here it is, decades later and I'm expecting him to bring the bird home like he had done before, but instead he used his foot to smash the bird. He humanely put the bird down, ending the animal's suffering. I was surprised because in my memories of Dad and birds it was only of him bringing injured ones home. This was something that seemed incongruous with old memories.

Do you remember Dad making kites? He made the best damn kites. He would get thin wood from apple crates, and would cover them with newspaper that he glued down with a flour and water paste. He built great big kites, four to five feet wide with a tail that was eight to ten feet long. The tails were made from knotted material and he would use twine for the kite string. He flew them right from our front yard. There were times he would not even leave the front porch and the kite was so far away that it would look like a pea in the distance. One time I remember the kite string breaking and Dad going all the way to Carroll College several miles from our house to retrieve the kite.

Yep, Les, you're right—the best damn kites.

CHAPTER FOUR

EARLY CHILDHOOD: THE SCHOOL YEARS

I was in second grade at St. Helena Grade School when I began stuttering. There was a Christmas play and every child in class had a line or two, and all of a sudden when it came to be my turn to perform, I froze and I could not say my line. Also in second grade, we had a split class. One of my teachers was Sister Rose Anthony, and she was just a mean bitch and particularly tough on me. She had no empathy for me and my stuttering. That's when a lot of belittling from people started for me—in the second grade.

My brothers and sisters did not tease me—sometimes Dad would tease but that was not traumatizing to me. What was traumatizing were my peers and the adults at the school teasing me. I know Mom stuttered when she was a little girl and Uncle Merlin stuttered, too. That was the one great regret Uncle Merlin shared with me, that he was so timid. Considering this, I think stuttering most likely has a genetic component.

In third grade I had Mrs. McGilten and she was a tough old bird. I raised my hand to answer a question and had to stand up. I froze and she belittled me in front of the class. From second grade on, the kids would take turns reading Dick and Jane stories and always when it came my turn to read, it was incredibly difficult and stressful and embarrassing—some of the kids would say, "You really stuttered bad that time."

Finally, my stuttering came to a head in the fourth grade and it was so bad I ran out of class and ran home. The strain got to me.

I had a great fourth grade teacher, Mrs. Murphy; she came to my house after lunch and took me back to class. In the car she asked me who was teasing me at school. She wanted specific names and details. She had me bring my guitar to school and asked me to play for the class. Then she asked me to play my guitar for the eighth grade class. While I was playing for the eighth grade class, she gave my classmates an earful. This forced the kids to not tease me, but there was still no help for my stuttering. Sympathy, yes, but still no help.

When I was in high school, at St. Helena High School, I did the thing I feared most and took speech. I was hoping that speech class would help me, but this nun who taught the class was brutal. She was a small, homely nun. She was very unsympathetic and had no idea what I was going through, so no understanding or sympathy from her. Before I would get up to give a speech in her class I would have huge beads of sweat on my body and my shirt would be soaked. A two-minute speech would take ten minutes. Since I did such an awful job, I got a C. In all my other classes I got straight As. It was torture; after class some of my classmates would say, "Boy, you struggled there." I wanted to reply, "Thanks for telling me, I never would have guessed, you must be psychic."

When I was going into my junior year of high school I was absolutely devastated when Dad said I had to go to public school because my older sisters would be going to college soon and attending Montana State University and that he and Mom could no longer afford to send all of us to Catholic school. Well, as it turned out, that was the best thing that ever happened to me. One thing I was determined to do was to continue to take speech classes at the public high school. So I get into public school and my speech teacher, Harry Smith, becomes one of the finest men I will ever meet. I spilled my guts to him; he was an actor, speech teacher, and was involved in drama classes and all that stuff—right at the get-go he was a sensitive guy. He had more sensitivity in his baby finger than an entire convent of nuns. I don't know if you should quote me on that, I may go to hell.

Mr. Smith's speech class was no better; it was torturous, same as

Catholic school. The product was the same except Mr. Smith gave me an A for effort; he did not care about the struggle. One day, my English Literature teacher, Mrs. Flanagan, held me back after class and very, very gently asked me about my stuttering. She asked if it would be okay if she contacted a speech therapist who worked for the district, and finally I got speech therapy when I was a senior in high school. My speech therapist was Bill Hickey; he was really, really good. He made me keep diaries when I stuttered to figure out what caused it. I just made up shit—by that time I was hanging out with Carla and I never stuttered with Carla. Maybe I never stuttered around Carla because I was too busy kissing her. Bill Hickey was trying to desensitize me, and he had me walk up to complete strangers and purposely stutter. What I realized was that 99 percent of people don't give a shit if you stutter, only I worried about stuttering.

Years later I ran into Mrs. Flanagan and thanked her for doing me such a great service. She was the first person who not only showed sensitivity but also had a plan to address it. She told me that she was worried that I was upset with her for referring me to a speech therapist. I assured her that I was not upset; she did the best thing for me that no other adult had ever done.

CHAPTER FIVE
LIVING THROUGH THE MUSIC

Jeannette, I know that Dad made Diane take piano lessons first and then Marlene because she was next in line. The girls didn't have any choice of musical instrument as far as I could see. But for some reason, Dad gave me a choice: piano or guitar. I would have liked to play both—but Dad could not afford it, so I chose guitar. Also, I heard classical music for two hours or more every day with my sisters playing the piano and I did not want to do that.

Interestingly enough, my first guitar teacher was Bob Bartmas—he taught me at two different times. The first time he taught me I was in fourth grade and my lessons continued for several years. During my guitar lesson I would watch Bob's fingers very carefully and later I would copy and imitate his hand movements. Bob thought he was teaching me music out of books, but I never learned anything about the music. He did not realize that I didn't actually comprehend the music, but my memory was good enough that I could practice what he was teaching me.

In fifth grade I joined the boys' choir that was headed by a priest named Father Hartman. I loved that guy. Gee, that was one class where I never had to worry about stuttering. Singing was my only relief. I never stuttered when I sang. In the boys' choir, stuttering was a total non-factor. I could carry a pitch. I think that is because I had guitar lessons and knew how to carry a tune. Father Hartman taught the boys' choir how to read music—the signatures, staff, timing, 2/2 time, 3/4 time, and what all of that meant. He had mnemonics for all of the lines and spaces of the music–you know, FACE, Good Boys Do Fine Always, etc. All of a sudden I started reading music in my guitar lessons and it started to come together. Singing in choir helped me understand the music.

I think I always had kind of a loud voice and that was preferable in choir. I think I hit my peak in sixth grade—I could hit a high A. I was at the top! Because I was in the choir I was lucky enough to go to Legendary Lodge Camp every summer; Legendary Lodge was on Salmon Lake in the Seeley/Swan area on Highway 83. The lake and camp sits right next to the Mission Range. The camp is still owned by the Diocese of Helena.

Mike and Rick were both in the choir also, so during the summer months we were able to go to camp together. When I was in the seventh grade I remember being on and working at Uncle Merlin's wheat farm. Aunt Jean cooked a lot of great food. After, Dad drove to Fort Benton to pick me up from the farm and then he drove me to Legendary Lodge for the camp. I was in choir for four years so I got to go to the camp for four years. It was great.

One thing the counselors did at the camp every year was scare the crap out of the boys for one night during the week. There would be guns firing off, and the camp counselors saying things like, "Someone was murdered," or "A bear broke into a cabin and ate someone!" We were scared to death and hid in our cabins. There was a theme every year and it was to teach the boys about communism—the communists put fear into their people and that is how they controlled them. There was always a lesson—you were not going to camp just to have fun—and it was something that we forgot about every year! Every year they were very convincing and very dramatic and the counselors threw themselves into their parts, changing the stories. One year I remember counselors saying the caretakers had gone nuts and were shooting people, etc. etc.

Oh my God, Les, what was wrong with those counselors? They sound crazy! Just a minute . . . I want to take a few deep breaths so my brain won't explode listening to this . . . whew . . . okay continue . . .

Well you know, this was during the Cold War and people were

so afraid of the communists. Remember Aunt Evike? She was a refugee from Hungary and the communist government there; she was always thinking that things were a communist plot. All of the boys at the camp were pretty poor learners. We just couldn't learn that lesson about communism well enough! At breakfast the next morning when we sat around long picnic tables heaped with great food such as pancakes, eggs, bacon, sausage, and biscuits, the counselors once again gave us the lecture about the evils and dangers of communism. As usual we got the lecture about the difference between democracy and communism. At the breakfast table I would think, "Oh yeah, now I remember! Tricked again by those camp counselors!!! Easily bamboozled—now, pass those pancakes!"

Even with that I loved camp—I was with a bunch of boys my own age and it is where I learned to swim, dive, water ski, bowl, play miniature golf, and make all kinds of crafts. It was lots and lots of fun. I also remember we got in long lines and passed firewood. The food was fit for kings and every meal was fantastic and all you could eat.

Over the years I had a bunch of guitar teachers. I remember a young guy named Larry; we went to the TV station and played guitar and after that we went to a recording studio and recorded the same music that we played at the local television station. Did you know that Helena has a recording studio?

So, do you remember Larry's last name or what song(s) you recorded?

No, it was too long ago and I don't recall what we played. I do remember Larry playing a Ventures' song, "Walk Don't Run," very well. Larry and I played music on the radio, TV, and performed at talent shows. Red Foley (the well-known radio DJ) emceed at the talent shows as well as another DJ, Johnny Little. He was a great big guy who took swills from a whiskey bottle that he kept behind the curtain—probably just to settle his nerves.

During the sixth and seventh grades I started to play in talent shows by myself in the Helena Civic Center auditorium. I would look out into the crowd—the auditorium was always packed at that time, standing room only. I felt very nervous but was okay once

I started playing and just looked at my Gibson.

I also took lessons from other guitar teachers as well, such as Larry Canoy and Chuck McDonald. Chuck gave me additional lessons on music theory. Later I took more lessons from my first teacher, Bob Bartmus, who taught me how to play by ear, to listen for chord changes and the subtle nuances of music. Larry Canoy taught me when I was really young and then again when I was older and a more advanced guitar player. He was my last teacher. Norm and Mark also took guitar from Larry, but Norm said he didn't like him. Larry was getting older and growing impatient. Larry expected Norm to play like me, which was totally unfair because I had already been playing guitar for five or six years.

Larry took me to play music for band jobs in Wolf Creek and many other towns and places. I played at schools and special events such as anniversaries and all kinds of functions. Larry was originally from St. Louis but moved his family to Wolf Creek because he did not want to raise his family in Missouri. In St. Louis he led a sixteen-piece band. His specialty was banjo. I went with him to play in bands throughout western and central Montana; I played with him up until he was in his 80s. I made $25 to $35 per night for these little gigs. Larry is the guy who helped me get used to playing in a band and playing in front of larger groups of people.

Around 1978 my friend Trev Thomas heard that Al Bock was looking for a guitar player for his Moonshine Band. I auditioned for the band and was accepted as their guitarist. When I joined Al's band they had a lot of jobs lined up, so we traveled all over the state to towns like Dillon, Butte, Ryegate, Deer Lodge, Anaconda, Townsend, Winston, Bozeman, East Helena, Fort Harrison (the Officer Club), and virtually every bar in Helena. We played at the Colonial, Jorgenson's, Nite Owl, Silver Spur, etc.

It was tough; I was not used to playing for four to five hours every Friday and Saturday night. During our short breaks I would go to the bathroom and hold my arm under hot water to get the feeling back in my arm and to help make it stop hurting. My left forearm was overworked to death. After the weekend band jobs my arm felt dead and ached for the next three to four days; it took at least six months for the pain in my arm to stop and my body to get used to it. I was forcing my palmaris longus, a one- to two-inch-long muscle between the palm and the wrist, to develop into a five-inch-long muscle. All guitar players have a pronounced Palmaris Longus from squeezing a guitar neck. All that pain started to pay off as I began to make between $6,000 to $10,000 per year just from the band jobs. I was able to buy all of my stereo equipment, new guitars, and put bread on the table.

Moonshine still practices one to two nights a week, because when you know thousands of songs, it's easy to forget the words, chords and chord progressions, the leads, or even the keys that the music was written in.

Hey Les, I always wondered why Moonshine quit hiring drummers and you guys started to use electric synthesized drums?

That's easy, because drummers got drunk and they sped up and slowed down; machines are rock steady and never change the tempo.

Talking about practicing takes me back to when I was a kid and remember that in the summer Dad made me practice four hours a day. I think Dad got that idea because Diane's voice teacher had a son who played the trumpet and his dad made him practice four hours a day. So that poor bastard had to practice four hours a day and Dad thought that was a good idea for me too. I went downstairs into the basement apartment (where Andy lives now) and used the table that Dad built out of extra material from the floor of the new house. Instead of practicing for four hours, I put together thousand-piece puzzles on that table. I always heard Dad when he was coming downstairs to check on me. When I heard him I would grab my guitar and start strumming. So during the summer I put together six to ten thousand- piece puzzles. I put together one puzzle a week. I'm sure Dad saw those puzzles coming together, but he never said anything. I think he was trying to keep me off the streets and running with my friends.

That's crazy . . . Les, those puzzles were difficult to put together!

Not when I had four hours a day to work on them! Just imagine how good I'd be at guitar if I had actually practiced four hours!

Here is a little story about how I managed to practice piano an hour everyday on school days and two hours a day on weekends, school breaks, and summer vacation. As you may remember, Mom and Dad bought a second piano and Dad put it in the living room of our new house a number of years before we actually moved in. It was a beautiful old piano, a Franklin Piano made in New York, with engravings on the front panel. It had a beautiful tone and a soft touch to the keys. I started piano when I was nine years old, probably was in the fourth grade. Karen Smith was my teacher and, of course, was Diane and Marlene's teacher as well. She was considered the best piano teacher in Helena. As I recall she was quite the ol' bitty. Mean and demanding comes to mind. Maybe she was a prison guard at Deer Lodge Penitentiary before deciding to become a piano teacher! Anyhow, she was so impatient, it was all classical-bassical with her. In her opinion all other forms of music seemed to be total nonsense, a total waste of time to study. All of my attempts at asking her if I could learn more modern music fell on deaf ears. I was quite determined, asking her a number of times when I was between the ages of nine and eighteen if I could play other types of music rather than just classical. Her response was always the same: No. Sometimes she said, "If you can play classical you can play anything." I found this to be completely untrue because years later when I first sat down to learn Gershwin's Preludes it felt like I was trying to read a foreign language.

There were times when Mrs. Smith got upset if I played the wrong notes and at times she hit my hands or forcefully put her hands on top of mine to play the correct notes. Of course as an adult looking back I realize that just because someone can play well does not mean that they should teach children; in my opinion she had no business being a piano teacher. One day—I think when I was around twelve or so—she began to make a move to slap my hands or force hers on top of mine (not an unusual thing for her to do) and I jerked my hands back and nearly fell off the piano bench! Well, she was surprised and never did that again. It was a good thing because

I think I was nearly at the age when I may have smacked her, plus I was nearly as big as she was.

As a little girl it was difficult for me to sit at the piano and practice non-stop for two hours. So I became very creative: I would run around the inside of our new house with my imaginary friends chasing me up and down the stairs; and I would pretend my best friend, Becky, and I were running around the house together. Also, I loved to sing so I stood on top of the piano bench and sang as loud as I possibly could to an imaginary audience. My favorite songs to sang were from the musicals South Pacific *and* Sound of Music. *I only heard the songs a very few times but, like you, I had a good memory for the music and words. My favorite song to sing was "Happy Talk Keep Talking Happy Talk," from* South Pacific. *Sometimes I played the songs by ear on the piano.*

When I heard Dad's loud steps coming into the house to check on me I, too, started playing—usually playing a classical piece really fast. Sometimes he said, "I want to see smoke coming out of that piano!" I used to fantasize about burning down the piano and then I could say to him, "See there is smoke coming out of that piano!" Anyway, despite all the dysfunction of being very afraid of Dad and just tolerating my piano teacher, I was learning to master Chopin, Mozart, Hayden, Bach, Beethoven, Grieg, etc. Somewhere during my early teens I actually did begin to learn to love the piano. There were times when Dad came into the house and said, "Okay, your two hours are up," and I just looked at him and said okay or said nothing. I became a master at not talking to him. Anyway, if I was learning a piece that I found very interesting or thought the music was beautiful, I kept on practicing so eventually there were times that I practiced three hours or more on a Saturday and/or a Sunday or on a day during my summer break.

Mrs. Smith sometimes said to me, "You have potential." The problem was she never explained to me what that meant, potential for what? If she meant as a concert pianist then she needed to explain to me what that meant. I later learned that what it meant is giving up your childhood and practicing a minimum of six hours a day. So if that had been explained to me at least I could have made a clear choice. I never understood what the expectations were and why all the practicing was required when all of my friends were running around having fun, going to movies, and meeting up to play on the weekends. What was the purpose of all the practicing? To be able to play the piano well? So what? In my teens I did realize that I had a skill that few of my peers possessed; some of my friends and even teachers were impressed when they heard me play. I was flattered, but to be honest I just wanted to be a kid.

So Les, as you can see, we were both mastering music in our own way; I with some of the great masters of classical music and you with the greats like Chet Atkins, Hank Williams, Merle Haggard, Marty Robbins, Johnny Cash, Ernest Tubb, and many other great country stars and composers from the 50s, 60s and 70s.

Jeannette, my real escape from all that practicing during the summer was working on Uncle Merlin's farm near Fort Benton. So, that practicing four hours a day was what gave me incentive to work on the farm—I was getting sick of putting puzzles together every summer and it was great because I could make money! I worked there between seventh and eighth grade and again after the tenth and eleventh grades. I met Carla in the eleventh grade and we were going together during the summers I was working for Uncle Merlin. I remember being with Uncle Merlin and Aunt Jean during the summer of '69 when man first walked on the moon.

Up until the time Carla, my wife, got sick, I always took my music for granted. I knew I was talented but I didn't have any feelings for my music. Once Carla got sick I became consumed with it. I thought about her illness 24/7. With music you have to put your full concentration into the music and you know that as well as I do. I had to put my full concentration in the songs—if I didn't I would forget the song—the words, leads, chords, etc. So this is when I realized the value of music—it was my therapy for brief moments. While playing I could forget about everything.

Since that time music has been much more important and emotional for me; once it dawned on me what it could do, it was easier for me to get lost in the music and my feelings. There were songs I had played in the band that I could not play for several years after Carla passed away. "Bye Bye Love" by the Everly Brothers was very hard to play without tearing up. When I first started playing it again, it was so emotional for me—maybe getting older and having a better perspective helps. As a teenage kid music had very little value, more like a punishment, but even then at times it could touch my soul. Now it can stomp on my soul.

So the point I am trying to make is that during the times Carla was sick and I was playing my band jobs, it was then that I realized the therapeutic value of the music. And you know that's when it dawned on me that it was an opportunity for my mind to get away from the ever-present thoughts about Carla dying.

Since the time Carla passed away I have stayed in the band. Strangely enough now, my favorite part of being in the band is practicing, so I've done a complete 180-degree turn with my feelings about practicing. When you're in a band, practicing is the least pressure that you're faced with. Practice is relaxing; you can work on the pieces of the song that are not finely tuned. When you are performing, the pressure is constant to play your best for every song, so at the end of each set you are physically and mentally drained. Plus, it is so much work to haul all the equipment to the jobs—just a lot of hard work.

So that is one of my favorite parts, the practicing, because it is the least stressful part of the music. It is always fun to learn new songs and new parts and hear something and become better and better with practice.

CHAPTER SIX

. . . FOR WE WALK BY FAITH, NOT BY SIGHT
(2 Corinthians)

Musically, I have been branching out a little—from playing in the band to playing Christian music. I participated in a Walk during 2009. A Walk is a retreat for men sponsored by Protestants and Catholics who have joined together in the Emmaus Society. It's a joint relationship between many Protestant denominations and the Catholic Church. The Catholics call it a Cursio; the Protestants call it a Walk. I had been asked by several people for years if I had any interest in doing a Walk, and for years I turned them down.

Baby Carla was born in April 2007 to Jenny and Bobby and named after her sweet grandmother, Jenny's mom. In 2009, she was ready to have her third and final heart surgery to correct her left hypoplastic heart congenital birth defect. (There's more on her story later.) I saw the Walk as an opportunity to pray for a successful heart surgery. When I find myself in a position of helplessness, the only thing that I can do is pray. And so I made a Walk in March of 2009 at St. Paul's United Methodist Church in Helena. The men making the Walk are called pilgrims, and there were over twenty pilgrims that year.

There were some musicians who played while I was making my Walk. I saw some spare guitars and I went and plunked on one of the guitars. On the fourth day of the Walk, which is a Bible study, I was invited many times by people to join their group. One of the fourth-day group members asked me to participate in the music group for the men's Walk to Emmaus and also to play for the closing session of the women's Walk.

This is just another way that my music has become such a significant part of my life. I can use my music in many ways, not just by playing in bars. I have branched off and am playing Christian music—this is new music for me, and a lot of this music is quite powerful and very spiritual. It fits the setting of the Walk beautifully. I am playing with several other guitarists and can quickly learn the music.

When it became known that I was at the Walk to pray for my granddaughter who was having open heart surgery, I was approached by Marty Martin, one of the pilgrims who was also the Blackfeet Indian chief and shaman (a medicine man) from the Blackfeet Indian Reservation in Browning, Montana, near Glacier National Park. Unbeknownst to me, he made a sweetgrass prayer braid for baby Carla. Where he got the sweetgrass I don't know, must have been in his medicine bag. He also had an eagle's wing, wolf pelt, and sacred tobacco. Anyway, during the Walk one day he presented me with the prayer braid. He had passed it around among everyone involved, which at that time was around 100 people, and they had all prayed with the sweetgrass braid. The chief presented it to me, an act that was very powerful—kind of a moving thing.

When the Walk was over, the following month he called me up to ask me what were baby Carla's favorite colors (keep in mind that she was two at the time). I told him I did not know and that Carla and I had talked about lots of things but that is one conversation we had never had so I had to get back to him on that. So I called up Jenny and said, "Do you have any idea what Carla's favorite colors are?" Jenny said "No, but my favorite colors are pink and purple and Carla doesn't mind if I dress her in pink and purple. So I'm guessing those are her favorite colors as well." So I called up the chief and I told him that we came to the consensus that Carla's favorite colors were pink and purple and he said, "Okay, that's what I needed to know." Later we set up a time for him to come to my house with Jenny, Bobby, Carla, Cody, Mom, and Marlene. Marty Martin lives in Valier on the edge of the Blackfeet Reservation near Browning. He and his wife, Vicki, drove down here to see us and in the meantime he had contacted some Christian outfit in Los Angeles, California, and they made a great big purple and pink prayer shawl for Carla. Marty gave the shawl to Carla at my house. He gave a special blessing for Carla and also for Marlene because she had recently lost her husband, Tom. He brought out an eagle's wing that he used during the blessings along with the wolf pelt and the sacred tobacco. He sprinkled out the sacred tobacco in the four directions: north, south, east, and west. It was to bless the ground and it was part of the blessing for Carla and Marlene.

This all comes back to Frances and Carl (baby Carla's great-great-grandparents). They were great lovers of Native American artifacts. I had a large suitcase that once belonged to Frances and Carl; it was stuffed with Native American leggings made with thousands and thousands of little beads, a medicine rattle with an eagle feather, and long, multicolored ribbons—the types you might see flying in the wind on top of teepees. I had additional paraphernalia and also three full Indian headdresses completely covered with eagle feathers. All of this Indian artwork and clothing dated back to the 1920s.

I decided to give Marty all of the Indian antiques for coming down to Helena to pray for my granddaughter. Marty was very surprised that I had all of these things and that I was giving them to him. He researched all of the things I gave him, and some of the Indian artifacts were from the Plains Indians and the Sioux and the Lakota tribes as well. Marty got together with the elders of his tribe and authenticated everything I gave him—they were all authentic Indian artwork and artifacts. There was also a pipe in the suitcase; however, it was broken. Marty was instructed by other Indian chiefs to take the pipe to a sacred place on a mountain in Glacier National Park and bury it.

Marty told me that when he passes on he will give all of the Indian artifacts to the Blackfeet Indian Reservation museum in Browning. I wanted to give everything to Marty because he was somebody who appreciated its value. This was my way of giving back to him because of his involvement in praying for the success of Carla's surgery. I gave the sweetgrass braid that Marty gave me during my Walk to Jenny and she keeps it above Carla's bed.

Attributed to an unknown Native American author
Poem shared by Phil Gottfredson

My father's face is in the rock on the
Mountain; the rock to which I turn
And all sons turn to see the face of all our fathers on the mountain.
The voice of my father is on the wind
And my voice also when it becomes strong
For only my sons to hear and keep on hearing after I am gone.
To fly higher than the eagle, to run faster
than the deer, to swim as freely as the
fish, to have the cunning of the coyote
and the sleekness of the lion—this is to
possess the spirit that sings in the wind
and cries in the fire, the spirit that shall never leave my home.

CHAPTER SEVEN
MEMORIES OF DAD

Mom and Dad going to school at Northern Montana College in Havre, Montana, had a profound impact on me. Dad died up there. I knew he had heart issues because when he came to visit us on Ferry Drive he wanted to walk around the property. The last few times he came out to visit us he could only walk a very short distance before he had to stop. He would stop to catch his breath and pop a nitro pill or two. I think Dad had known for at least ten years that his heart was bad, but at the same time he chose to not address those problems. Back in those days heart bypasses were pretty new and he wasn't willing to try any newfangled procedure. I don't know if he just didn't have any faith in how they worked or if he thought that somehow he would be incapacitated and wind up in a wheelchair or something. I never talked to him about his heart or his health—I don't recall talking to Dad at all about personal issues.

Yes, he was very quiet and would not discuss his health problems with any of us.

That's true; it never occurred to me that there could be any kind of fatal weakness concerning Dad. He never showed weakness about anything. Dad was very private when it came to his personal issues and never steered the conversation when he came to visit. When he did visit he always came bearing food, donuts, or ice cream or some dang thing, never coming empty-handed. During his visits we talked, but I always talked about my struggles or about my family and me. So the topic was never about Dad or his issues.

I was sure impressed by Dad when he retired from the ASARCO Smelter in East Helena. After just a couple of weeks of retirement, he went back to school. (I think he retired just to catch up on sleep because he had changed shifts every two weeks for thirty years.) I never guessed that Dad wanted to go back to school as he never spoke to me about it. He never said, "When I retire I am going back to school." I just figured he and Mom would do more traveling.

When he went back to school in 1976, in Helena, Montana, he entered an adult education program, where he started with the third grade. In Okmulgee, Oklahoma, Dad did complete school through the eighth grade. He quit school and got a job with his dad in a glass manufacturing company. This was during the Depression and Dad's family were quite poor during that time. There were nine children in the family and he was the oldest son. So he took responsibility to help bring needed money into the family. He decided to begin his studies with early elementary school because he was concerned he missed a great deal of the basics as a child.

When attending the adult education program Dad walked back and forth to school every single day. He never drove and even walked when it was 30 below zero. When I was driving home I sometimes saw him walking. Each time I stopped and asked him if he wanted a ride, Dad hopped in the car and let me give him a ride home. He went to school every day for three years to get his GED before he and Mom went to Havre for college.

Years later I met Dr. Tom Carlin at the Broadwater Athletic Club, the guy who ran the adult education program that Dad attended. Over time we developed a friendship and I started talking to him about Dad and how I was raised. I told him about Dad going back to school and starting back in the third grade after retiring from the smelter. That's when Dr. Carlin asked my father's name. It turned out that he knew Dad because he was the head administrator for Adult Education; he had just completed his doctorate at that time and that was one of his very first jobs. Dr. Carlin would tell me stories about Dad at that school and how the other students, who were much younger, looked up to him. It was nice to hear positive stories about Dad.

Dad, of course, at age fifty-four was the oldest one there because most of the people working on getting their GEDs were high school dropouts. He arrived at school every day no matter what the weather was like—he was there like clockwork. Dr. Carlin explained that Dad was an inspiration to the students who were struggling and often felt like quitting but saw the determination of this older man there every day, which encouraged them not to quit and to do what it took to get their GED. Dr. Carlin said that there was one student who had very poor hygiene. He reeked and smelled so bad that the other students complained about his smell. The teachers and administrators, including Dr. Carlin, tried talking to him but they didn't have any effect. But because all of these young people looked up to Dad, Dr. Carlin asked him to talk to this kid about his hygiene. So Dad did and the kid smelled like a rose from that point on. No one was privy to the conversation between these two. So I can only guess about how the conversation went; my guess is the conversation was just pointing out that the kid was not doing himself any favors by not being clean and how his smell was distracting other students. However the conversation went, it was persuasive, and this kid started taking care of himself. It was probably the first time in this kid's life that someone he respected talked to him and told him that for his own sake he needed to change his ways.

After Dad got his GED, he and Mom packed up and left for Havre, Montana. I have a funny mental picture of Mom and Dad going off to school. They were packing up the truck; Dad had taken off the camper so they could take everything they needed to furnish their dorm. It reminded me of *The Beverly Hillbillies,* my God he had that thing loaded down.

They moved to Havre so they could both attend Northern Montana College. *Mom had graduated high school in Fort Benton, Montana. She wanted to attend college as much as Dad. Mom studied history, French, and theology. She loved history and theology and her first language was French. She heard her French grandparents (from St. Alexander, Quebec) speaking primarily French in the house when she was growing up, so she and her sister*

Bernadine and brother Merlin were quite fluent in French as young children. I am not certain how well they could speak it but they understood it very well. I remember as a child Mom using sweet French words when talking to us.

Mom and Dad attended college for a year and a half or so. I remember taking my family up there and visiting with them over the weekends—I remember talking to Dad about how school was going; he was going to school only because it was something he wanted to do. He wasn't doing it to further a career or land some type of job. He was just doing it because he was interested in learning. Dad told me about a teacher who prodded him to do something faster or in a different way in one of his classes. Dad only did so much as far as homework went, in his studies in diesel mechanics. Perhaps Dad was going too slowly through the textbooks or his lab work. Anyway Dad said he had to set the teacher straight. My interpretation from the little bit that Dad said was that he let him know that he wasn't there looking for a job or a career—he was just there to learn and he was going to learn at his own pace. He basically told this guy to get off his ass. *Mom, however, did not have any conflicts with her teachers! Both were great students and were getting straight As.*

I remember Mom telling me how much she really enjoyed college and meeting all the students in her classes and her teachers. She was always very patient with Dad and understood the trauma WWII had on him and how it affected his everyday life. Such as being impatient at times, quick to anger, and needing to help himself stay calm by listening to country music or classical. He loved both. Even though Dad seemed to be the one "calling all the shots" when we were growing up, I think Mom always had his ear and he would listen to her suggestions. I have vivid memories when we were growing up of Mom helping Dad with reading. He would read the local newspaper, Time *magazine, and* Newsweek *cover to cover. He frequently would stop to ask Mom what a word was—she would tell him and explain the meaning, then he would continue reading. Clearly a lack of education does not equate with ignorance. Dad was extremely intelligent and I believe under different circumstances he could have been anything. Mom, too, growing up during the Depression certainly affected her future educational choices.*

I agree. It's an inspiration that Mom and Dad lived in married student housing, as they were the oldest couple in the apartments. Dad always kept a big box of fruit in the house and all of the kids often came around and grabbed a piece of fruit from Mom and Dad. Right after Dad died in November 1981, the school created a children's park beside the married student dorms called the R. O. Morgan Park. He and Mom made a lot of friends the year and a half that they were there. The families, including the children, who lived in married student housing liked our parents—so much that they named a children's park in his honor.

CHAPTER EIGHT

DAD AND THE WWII 1ST SPECIAL SERVICE FORCE

D ad was an honest man but he was not a refined kind of guy; he was really crude and rough around the edges. His honesty was unshakable—he never cheated anyone out of a dime. Being in the war, working at the smelter for thirty years, and, of course, genetics contributed to his stress levels. He was really good at holding grudges and that, too, contributed to the stress of his life. I think it was really tough for him to forgive and that he was beginning to explore that challenge when he and Mom were in Havre going to school. One time when Mom and Dad went to church the priest said something about not being able to get into heaven if you cannot learn to forgive. When they got home Dad asked Mom if she thought he could get into heaven. It was tough for him to be able to forgive anybody who crossed him.

I know for a fact that his brother, Uncle Norman, never crossed him. *Dad and Uncle Norman were very close.*

Uncle Norman was a great guy. Dad never appreciated stories about himself, especially stories that were about him when he was young because he thought that people embellished the stories.

He was a very private person at heart and simply did not want to discuss much about his early life, the war, or especially any emotions or feelings.

Have you heard of the Gramm-Rudman-Hollings Act? This act took away Social Security benefits for retired railroad workers. Uncle Norman worked thirty-seven years for the railroad and could only just scratch out a living after he retired because of this federal act. Both Uncle Norman and Dad worked very hard their entire lives to make a decent living for themselves and their families.

Dad and all of his siblings were so generous with all of us in regards to time and taking such great care of us when we visited them. They were very affectionate, loving, and friendly people. They seemed very happy to see all of six of "Bud's" kids and were always so kind to us. I have wonderful memories of all of my aunts, uncles, and sweet cousins. The large Morgan clan is full of amazing people who really understand affection and love.

Dad's family came from the heart of the country. The family started in Melbourne, Arkansas, and Big Cabin, Oklahoma, and while there survived the Depression and the Dust Bowl. The hard life he had as a child may have helped make him a really strong and determined individual, and probably explained why he was such an exemplary soldier. Dad knew how to survive.

Dad was a WWII veteran. He and Uncle Ralph were both part of the 1st Special Service Force—a regiment of American and Canadian soldiers. He was seventeen years old when he joined the service; he was in the Army from 1939 until he was discharged in July 1945. Dad trained at Fort Harrison, in Helena, Montana, and served under Colonel Frederick. During the war he fought in thirteen major battles and campaigns in Italy, France, Belgium, and Germany (including the Rome-Arno, Ardennes-Alsace, and Rhineland campaigns). Dad was injured three times during his WWII service.

He was awarded the following medals and ribbons:
    General Order (GO) 40 WD45 Central;
    Europe: GO 48 WD45 Southern France;
    Aleutian Islands: GO 33 WD45 Naples – Foggia;
    American Defense Service Ribbon;
    Good Conduct Medal;
    Purple Heart: GO 73 HQ36 General Hospital 44;
    Distinguished Unit Badge GO 31 HQ 3BUSA 45;
    AP Service Ribbon;
    2 Bronze Service Stars;
    EAME Service Ribbon;

Silver Star (also known as the Silver Service Star);
Lapel Button Issued for the Presidential Citation 501st Airborne,
a Regiment of the 101st Airborne;
13 Battle Service Ribbons;
On February 3, 2015, Congress awarded members of the
1st Special Service Force the Congressional Gold Medal.

Dad was well known as a very good soldier and marksman. Canadian Andy Olsen, a good friend of Dad's who served with him in Europe, once stated at a 1st Special Service Force reunion, "Your Dad was the Nazi's worst nightmare come true." Andy was one of three guys who approached Mom at a reunion and said, "Your husband saved my life three times." Another said, "Your husband was the best shot in the whole outfit," and yet another 1st Special Service Force soldier said, "Your husband was the bravest son-of-a-bitch that I ever knew."

Back in 2002 Andy Olsen wrote a letter about Dad. This may have been when Mom donated Dad's M1 semi-automatic rifle, his personal gun throughout the war, to the Military Museum at Fort Harrison in Helena, Montana. To quote Andy, "I have shot with a lot of people and I have seen some of the best riflemen, but Morgan was the top one as far as I'm concerned."

Dad had perfected a technique called speed shooting, which consisted of firing off eight rounds as quickly as possible, and that skill made him a great soldier. When I read that letter it reminded me of Uncle Norman and the times that he went deer hunting with Dad. Uncle Norman said, "It wasn't any fun hunting with R.O. because the deer had six or eight bullets in its head before it hit the ground." I think this may have made Uncle Norman feel bad for not being such a good shot. So I think Dad demonstrated his technique for firing and Uncle Norman was not able to do that. Also, Dad was using his M1 semi-automatic rifle and Uncle Norman was using a standard 30-06.

All of us, Mom, Dad's children, and people who knew him as a soldier recognize that he was a hero. We cannot imagine what he experienced as a soldier and a sergeant. He fought with unbelievable, undaunting courage and strength to help save the world from the tyranny of Hitler and Mussolini. His medals and ribbons tell the story.

Thanks to Dad's sacrifice as well as many other brave soldiers and sailors, we are living free today. We can only hold our deepest gratitude and thanks for Dad's service and the brave and amazing Armed Forces service men and women of WWII.

For further reference, Les and I recommend to our readers the following books: The First Special Service Force *by Lieutenant Colonel Robert Burhans and* The Last Fighting General: The Biography of Robert Tryon Frederick *by Anne Hicks.*

It is really important for us to remember that Mom and Aunt Bernadine prayed every day for four years for Dad and Uncle Ralph to survive the war. I'm sure they dedicated many Masses to them as well. I believe the Lord answered their prayers—I'm not sure why or how it happened but somehow they both survived.

On July 13, 2014, Aunt Bernadine and Mom's very dear friend, Tina Hash, said, "I always thought Bernadine and Georgie were two angels walking on the Earth."

Hi Dad, I have been thinking about you a lot these days and I know that you are at peace in Heaven. I've been thinking about a song that I am sure you'll remember. I am dedicating it to you.

"We'll Meet Again"
By Ross Parker and Hughie Charles, 1939

We'll meet again
Don't know where
Don't know when
But I know
We'll meet again
Some sunny day

Keep smilin' thru
Just like you
Always do
'Til the blue skies drive
The dark clouds
Far away

And will you please say hello
To the folks that I know
Tell 'em that I won't be long
And they'll be happy to know
That when you saw me go
I was singing this song

We'll meet again
Don't know where
Don't know when
But I know
We'll meet again
Some sunny day

So Honey
Keep on smilin' thru
Just like you always do
'Til the blue skies
Drive the dark clouds
Far away

And would you please say hello
To all the folks that I know
And tell 'em I won't be long
They'll be happy to know
That when you saw me go
I was singing this song

We'll meet again
Don't know where
Don't know when
But I know
We'll meet again
Some sunny day

CHAPTER NINE

FIRST LOVE

W ell, when it comes to Carla, the first time I laid eyes on her I was about sixteen and a half years old after I transferred to public school in the middle of my junior year. It was at the very end of 1967, probably in December, sometime before Christmas. By that time she would have just turned seventeen and I was still sixteen; she was about seven months older than me. We met at the ice-skating rink in Helena, probably on a Saturday. I was there with my friend Terry. Terry had transferred from Plains, Montana, and I had just transferred to public school, so on the very first day of school that winter semester, both of us were wandering the halls trying to find out where a particular class was, and it turned out we had many of the same classes. So from our very first day we became friends; we were the only ones each of us knew. We both played guitar and started spending most of our free time and weekends together.

So, for whatever reason we had gone to the ice-skating rink, and Terry was always on the lookout for girls. Terry spotted Carla and Shirley, and Shirley turned out to be his future wife. Actually, I don't think Shirley was there—maybe another friend of Carla's. Terry was trying to pair up with Carla. He always kind of led the show when it came to girl chasing, so he started chucking snowballs at Carla and her friend and they started throwing snowballs back. We started hanging around those girls and when it came time to leave we left about the same time they did. Terry and I started to follow the girls home in his car, and eventually Carla drove home and Terry followed her right to her house. Her Dad wasn't there. Anyway, Carla let us in and she was with a girlfriend. Carla had the latest Beatles album, *Sgt. Pepper's Lonely Hearts Club Band*, and we sat around and listened to that. We listened to the album a couple of times and then Terry and I took off.

Unbeknownst to me, Carla's dad, Jim, had a rule: there were to be no boys in the house if he wasn't there. If I had known that I wouldn't have gone into the house. Jim Harrington, who had been in bands since the time he was fifteen, played regularly at the Diamond S in Boulder, Montana, so that's where he was that night. Carla didn't mention the fact that boys were not supposed to be in the house when her dad was gone.

Anyway, after meeting Carla I started noticing and paying attention to what classes she might have in school. Also, I remember that there was a dance coming up or some kind of event that was going on at the civic center. There was a gal (a well-known singer) who sang "Just Call Me Angel of the Morning" and, of course, Terry always took the lead, so we went to the concert at the civic center. Prior to the concert I did not have the nerve to ask Carla to go to the concert so Terry asked her for me. Carla said, "No, I won't go with him, he has to ask me himself." I was too nervous or shy to ask her myself and I also hated to talk on the phone because I stuttered so badly. Anyway, I was forced to call her and talk to her on the phone myself. I think Terry just gave me the phone when she said she would not go to the concert unless I talked to her myself. When I did talk to her she said yes, she would like to go. So that was our first date and I was basically forced to talk to her and ask her out, and you know I don't think I had ever done that with a girl before. So that kind of started the relationship between Carla and me, and after that I started talking to her much more often.

Because Terry had a car, after school it was inevitable that we drove by Carla's house to see if she was there, and if she was, she would open the door and let us in. This was after school and before Jim got off work. One time we happened to be inside the house when Jim got home from work, and he walked in and started chewing Carla's ass out about having boys in the house when he was not home. She knew she had broken the rules and we had to leave right away. So that is the day I found out about the rules—no boys in the house! Jim was very upset that Carla had broken the rules. As it turned out I went with Carla for a whole entire year before Jim knew me long enough to let me come into the house without him being there. A whole entire year! So, finally there was a Saturday where Jim was playing a band job at the Diamond S Ranch and I was allowed to be in the house when he wasn't there. That day Carla's sister, Georgia, came home with her husband, Mike. I had never laid eyes on them before. Mike Drake was in the Navy, stationed in San Diego, but he had also been stationed on a ship off the coast of Vietnam. He was on leave and he and Georgia drove home to Helena from San Diego. So anyway, this was the first night that I was allowed to be in the house. When Georgia came in she started jumping all over Carla because she had a boy in the house, and she ran me out of the house after I waited for a whole year to get into the house! So needless to say, I didn't think a lot of Georgia, that's for sure. She didn't believe Carla when she told her that I had permission to be there and I was in no position to stand my ground with someone I had never seen before, so I left.

When Mike was on leave, he and Georgia were in Helena for a few weeks. I remember Carla and me driving together with them to the Diamond S to see their dad play. So I got to know Mike and Georgia somewhat.

It didn't take long for me to fall in love with Carla, and soon I was talking to her on the phone for hours every night. And before long I was eating dinners at her house, actually more often than I was eating at home. It wasn't very long before I was seeing her almost every day.

I want to tell you one funny story. The folks knew about Carla and I'm not sure if they had met her, but I'm assuming I had introduced her to them. You know, most of the time (except when it was time to study for tests or homework) I was off seeing Carla. Each time that I visited Carla I told Dad that I was going to the library with Terry; it wasn't that I was scared to tell Dad but I just figured that he didn't need to know that I was with Carla. So one night, after the second or third time that I went to visit Carla, I told Dad once again that I was going to the library. Dad said, "I know that you're going to see that girl! You don't need to tell me that you're going to the library; I know you're seeing Carla so don't tell me you're going to the library." I said, "Okay, I won't lie to you about that anymore." Dad knew what Terry was all about. He was a tall, good-looking, strapping kid with a car, and he knew there was one thing on our minds and it wasn't the library, it was girls! Dad knew exactly what was going on and, you know me, a stupid, naive sixteen-year-old kid—I thought I could fool him. When you're that age you never take into account that the older generation has any wisdom.

So from that time on, which was pretty much at the beginning of my relationship with Carla, I had to be straight with Mom and Dad; there was no more bullshitting about where I was going. I would just say, "I'm going to see Carla." So then I began introducing Carla to the family and the relatives and I'm sure it was about that time that she met you. I took her to the Randall's house and introduced her to Uncle Ralph, Aunt Bernadine, and cousins Dan, Rick, Mike, and Steve. This was before Danny got sick so he was doing really well at that time. I think Steve was only around six or seven years old.

So that is when Carla started to get to know my family. I don't think she really got to know Diane well at that time because Diane was already off to college. Mark was really young then; Mark took a shine to Carla and Carla took a shine to him. She would take Mark out for hamburgers and Cokes at Gerties on Last Chance Gulch. Mark was kind of a rough little kid then; sometimes he had a really foul mouth, as you may recall, and he was not always easy to deal with. He was really busy and everything. Carla was good with Mark and he would behave himself with her.

I remember Carla as the first and only person I talked to without stuttering—that is how comfortable I was around her. You know she must have been falling in love with me about the same time as I was falling in love with her. I don't recall any type of crazy shit happening that would make us want to break up or anything, you know, we didn't have big fights about anything. I think that she had maybe two boy-friends before me; I don't think it was very serious. These boys gave me a hard time in school though, but Terry was always there to put the kibosh on that and I guess he was kind of like my bodyguard too. I probably only weighed 120 pounds and everybody at Helena High School thought I was a freshman but I was a junior. Carla and I were both small. So as Carla and I got closer it was tremendously exciting to start kissing her and she kissed me right back. And we spent so much time kissing in a car in front of Shirley's parents' house that they com-plained. They wanted us to go someplace else! I remember one time being in Carla's car, and it was somewhere close to downtown and we were parked near a substation. This one was somewhere near 14th Street. There was a big lightning storm going on and we were kissing in the car and that dang substation got hit by lightning right next to us. It scared the heck out of us! It was very loud.

At this same time Carla was bringing me around to introduce me to her side of the family. Her grandparents, Carl and Frances, were living in the house that I'm living in now. When Jim found out that I played guitar he asked me to come over to his house and play with him and his friend Jim. I don't know if I did that great of a job, but I did my best to play standards with the two Jims who were both great musicians. So I think he started to like me a lot and have respect for me.

I think the first big thing that came along for Carla and me was in the spring, our junior prom. That was the first formal dance that I had ever been to. I have a picture that Jim must have taken. When I see that picture I see this skinny little guy with these black, horn-rimmed glasses and braces on my teeth! Yeah when I look at this picture of us, I see Carla and me as two little kids. But you know, you don't think of yourself as a little kid at the time. I think it is good that young people see themselves as grown-ups because if they didn't they might scare themselves out of making any decisions. To me, it's a good thing that young people view life with an open mind and look forward to the possibilities it holds. When you are sixty it's not that you don't look on life with a positive view, but you wonder how you could have been so naïve about life. You had no idea what was in store. But somehow you made it through and made a life, you know, you made it to the point where you are right now. Youth is something that there is no shortcut from experiencing; you have to live through it. You just wish that you knew a little bit of what might come, but there is no shortcut from that. You just have to live through it.

Before I continue with my story of Carla it is important to point out that just the simple act of throwing a snowball at someone affected my entire life, and I am talking about every aspect of my life. That not only started my road of marriage and children and everything that goes with that, but it also set me up with my life's career. After the junior prom we continued dating and seeing each other as often as we could, and before long the senior prom came along and I remember going to that and the all night senior party. I don't think we wanted to be separated from each other so we both decided that Carroll College in Helena would be the best way to make that happen. My freshman year at Carroll College, taking pre-med courses was extremely hard; I remember taking a physics course that I needed help with. I got some help from Jim. So that is when Jim thought that I might go into engineering.

I know, he saw firsthand your quick math brain and probably wondered why did your dad want you to be a doctor?

Maybe! So rather than go back to the farm in the summer, Jim thought that I should work for his firm and learn more about civil engineering. When I was in college, I was offered a job by her dad, who was working for Engineering Corporation of America, an engineering firm that later became Stahly and Harrington, eventually becoming Stahly Engineering and Associates. Over the course of five years I worked for all three of those companies. But you know that all started with Jim who gave me a job that turned into a lifelong career. In 1975 I began working for the City of Helena in the Engineering Department and stayed with them until I retired. So it turns out that that snowball actually "snow-balled" into life-changing events for me. Little did I know at the time that I was changing the entire direction my life would take. Up until that time I had never had a girlfriend and the only work I had done was on Uncle Merlin's farm.

Carla and I had been seeing each other for over two years. Even though we were only eighteen and nineteen years old at the time, we had talked about the possibility of getting married. We didn't know for sure when that would happen, we just knew that it would. We had become very close by then. So it was in the summer between our freshman and sophomore year at Carroll College that Carla was late for her period and it was apparently quite regular. She became quite concerned when it was late. Carla went to the doctor who ran some tests. I remember her coming to me and telling me she was pregnant. I was home at the time and I remember her being very shocked and seeming really concerned. I know I was a little bit shocked! This was forty-one years ago, so the details are not precise at this time; however, I do recall talking about what we should do and we quickly decided that Carla was going to keep the baby and we would get married. For me, marrying her was just the natural thing to do. We had talked about getting married, we did not know how and when, but all of a sudden now we knew how and when. The how was as quickly as possible and the when was even quicker. We decided right then and there that we needed to let our parents know what was going on.

I figured that I needed to join the Navy to support my family so I decided that that's what I would do. At that time the Vietnam War was in full bloom. I had already been through the lottery for the draft and knew that I wasn't going to be drafted by the Army because my number was too high; there were 365 numbers in the barrel, and July 10 was 158 and the cut-off was 150. I went to college with guys who were number one. I was relieved to not be drafted into the Army because I would have gone to boot camp then directly to Vietnam. I thought the Navy was a good choice for serving, so my plan was to drop out of college and join the Navy. Carla would have to come and live on a naval base and I would be out to sea.

Those were our plans when we went to talk to our parents. The first one we talked to was Carla's dad, Jim. I think he was outside working on an old surveying instrument—you know Jim, when he was working on anything he always used his full concentration and didn't like to be interrupted. So I went outside and was the one to tell him that Carla and I needed to talk to him. He asked if it could wait and I said no, we needed to talk to him now. So he grudgingly came into the house. Carla did most of the talking when it came to her dad and she said, "I'm pregnant." Right away Jim followed the train of thought that this was something that could be taken care of—meaning an abortion. I don't recall too much lecturing to Carla because that wouldn't have changed anything. Right away Carla added that our plans were to get married. Jim didn't think that was such a good idea mainly because we were young, still in school, you know, all of the logical reasons. Jim was all about rational logic. He had been through three wives and had been through quite a struggle raising his two daughters. So he just couldn't see where we were in any kind of position to get married. He tried his best, using logic to convince Carla and me that there was no way that we should even think about getting married and that the best thing to do was to have an abortion and handle it that way. But Carla was hearing none of it. There was no way she was going to do that.

So when Jim knew that he couldn't change our minds, his idea was to go up to Carl and Frances's house and they would back him up. Carla, of course, was very, very close to her grandmother; she was the dominant female in her life. Frances, of course, was the queen bee; she pretty much had say over her entire clan including Jim and his daughters. She had a lot of influence and she was very good to Jim, Carla, and Georgia. Jim was sure that Carl and Frances would back him. And he was half right. When we got to the house Carl and Frances were both at home. Carla did most of the talking; they were her family. I stood next to Carla of course. I really didn't say much, but, you know, I had already done my part and everybody knew it. If I said anything at all it was my plan to join the Navy. Jim explained how he thought it was best if we got an abortion. You know, Carl was so emotional that he got his coat and with tears in his eyes he looked at Carla and said, "I hate to say it but I agree with your dad." Then he left. But Frances, on the other hand, was in complete agreement with Carla, that the best thing for us to do was to get married. She said, "You'll have a lot of help," and also said, "We weren't in this alone." That was the first moment of support that we had in this trial by fire. We thought that maybe this might work. Frances didn't think that we were too young, in college, etc., she just disagreed with everything that her son had said. So at that point Jim knew that the only thing he could do was to join in with his daughter and mother's decision. Then he said something that totally surprised me. He said, "Well, if they're going to get married then I will put Les through Carroll; I will pay for his college." So then it was two down and one to go. From there we went over to Mom and Dad's house.

When we got to Mom and Dad's I told them that we needed to talk to them and asked them to sit down. This time I did the talking and I said, "Carla is pregnant and we've decided to get married." The first thing that came out of Dad's mouth was, "Who's the father?" Well the next four words came out of Carla's mouth, in just as stern a voice as Dad's, and she stated, "Who do you think!" And then his tone softened up and he said, "Well, then I guess there's going to be a wedding." Then Dad said something that surprised me, too; he said, "You guys can live in the basement apartment." There hadn't been anybody in that basement apartment for many years. So we had all of the support and help that we needed from Carla's family and my family so that I did not have to join the Navy and I could still continue with my college education.

Mom did start talking to us and she asked if we could get married in the Catholic Church. So the next step was to talk to a priest. We talked to Father Dusseault of St. Helena's Parish. He was a relatively new priest. We set up a meeting within a few days and we went to his office and the first question that he asked me was, "Why do you want to get married?" The first thing that I blurted out was, "Well, first of all, she's pregnant!" He replied, "That's not a good reason." So I had to rephrase my answer to, "We love each other and she's pregnant!" And I emphasized to him that we had to get married right away, and he said that it required a six-week Pre-Cana course. I emphasized that if it was going to take six weeks I would go to a Justice of the Peace. He said, "Well, hold on a minute, maybe we can condense that a little to two weeks." I said okay because I was thinking we should get married tomorrow. I'm not really sure what Carla felt about getting married in the Catholic Church; I think we both just did it to appease Mom. Because I don't think it was really important to me to get married in the church.

Carla and I were married on a Thursday evening, September 3, 1970, at St. Helena's Cathedral in Helena, Montana. The reception immediately followed at Carla's grandparents, Frances and Carl Schiller's house. I remember Dad in a suit (a rare occurrence) and I'm sure there are many stories about the reception I don't recall but mainly I was so happy being married to Carla but with no idea what was in store. I had no doubt that somehow everything would work out.

When Carla and I got married we moved into the basement apartment on Hauser Boulevard that had been vacant for many years. It worked great for us especially since Dad and Mom didn't ask for any rent from us the entire time we lived there, about three years. After the wedding, I'm not sure what time we finally got home, but sometime between 7:00 A.M. and 8:00 A.M. we heard a pounding on the door; Dad was there with an armload of groceries. It was the first of a lot of groceries that we got from Mom and Dad that pretty much continued whenever Mom and Dad came to visit, up until Dad passed away. Dad may have lacked social abilities and could be crude, but he was one of the most honest and generous people to me and my family that I have ever known.

Adam was born March 20, 1971, at 10:14 A.M. Carla had been having contractions for most of the day on the 19th and felt like we should go the hospital at about 10:30 P.M. When Carla was admitted to the labor room I was not able to be with her since there were other women in labor at the time. I was able to be in a waiting room a short distance away, after having to wait in the main waiting area in a different part of the hospital for at least a few hours. I think both Mike and Rick Randall were with me when Carla was admitted but then went home as the hours dragged on. I finally had to go home about 8:00 A.M. to get a little sleep and someone called in a short time to tell me Carla was about to give birth or had already had Adam, I just can't remember for sure. Before Adam was born we had long and lively discussions about what to name our new daughter or son. If we had a boy, it was going to be Adam or Oscar. Oscar is the name of a box turtle Rick had gotten when he was about twelve years old and is still alive today! That's a great testament to Rick.

We lived in the basement apartment for three years until my father-in-law, Jim Harrington, went to Vietnam to do civil engineering work for his engineering firm. It was about this time that Carla became pregnant with Andy. She had already picked out a name that came to her in a dream so there was no discussion on that point. We moved into Carla's dad's house on Choteau Street to house-sit while Jim was out of the country. It was a beautiful house—it was a mansion compared to where we lived the first three years. I believe it was built in the 1880s; somebody had some money when they built that thing. Carla and I put in a garden at the house, it was the first time we planted corn and it was super tall and had a great yield. When Jim first got back from Vietnam we were all in that house for a short time. I remember Jim commenting on how sweet the corn was.

Also during our stay there Carla got our first dog, Chica. I was working out of town during the week and I would get back really late on Friday nights. When I went into the house one Friday all of a sudden this little dog was barking like crazy at me. I think we almost scared each other to death. This was the time before we had cell phones so I did not know about the dog. When Carla was growing up she always wanted a dog or cat but her dad said that when she grew up and got married she could have all the dogs and cats she wanted. So she took that to heart. You know she never asked me if I wanted an animal—she just brought them home. She was married and that meant she could have all the animals she wanted. If she had talked to me about it I probably would have said, "Oh, shit, we can't afford that!" She loved dogs and cats, always did.

During this time, while Carla was pregnant with Andy, I was working out of town in Eureka, Montana. One day an engineer from the main office drove up there to tell me Carla had given birth to Andy, they were both in the hospital and doing fine. This was a huge shock because Carla was only seven and a half months pregnant. Andy was only four pounds, six ounces when he was born on June 5, 1974. He was covered with embryonic hair and occasionally scared the crap out of us when he stopped breathing and turned a lovely shade of blue. He was kept in an incubator for two or three days before we were allowed to bring him home. I didn't know if Andy would survive or not, but the first time I saw him lying on his stomach in the hospital he lifted his head up and looked around, which impressed me. When we got him home we had to keep a close eye on Andy to make sure we rubbed his feet or cheeks whenever he stopped breathing. I think the hospital may have sent him home not knowing if he would live or die. I don't know if Carla got any sleep those first few months keeping such a close eye on Andy. When Andy was just a few months old Carla knew he didn't respond to sounds normally and seemed to be in his own world. It didn't take long to get the diagnosis of significant hearing loss. It took another twenty-five years to get the rest of his diagnosis.

When Carla's dad, Jim, came back from Vietnam, Carla got busy and found a new mobile home to buy that fit our budget and also a place to put it: Lump Gulch, near Clancy. I remember one day coming home to Lump Gulch and Carla running toward me and jumping into my arms and exclaiming, "Guess what, we're pregnant!" Andy was only five months old and this caught me by surprise, to say the least, but Carla was so excited. At about seven and a half months into her pregnancy, Carla started to have false labor pains, which spooked us because that was when she had Andy. They happened periodically and were twenty minutes apart for six weeks when they suddenly changed to ten minutes and getting closer. It was a twenty-minute ride to the hospital from Lump Gulch and Carla made me stop at a convenience store so she could buy some hard candy to suck on. I remember her doubling over with contractions several times in the store while she was deciding what particular candy to buy while I was crapping my pants. I think when we got to the hospital she was already dilated big time and had Jenny within twenty minutes. Our neighbors took turns fixing us dinner each night for the first week that we were home—how cool and generous.

Shortly after Jenny was born on August 3, 1975, Carl Schiller gave us an acre of ground in the valley. With his help we got a well drilled and a septic tank and drain field installed and moved the trailer out there. Dad paid for a foam insulating company to come out and foam the walls of the trailer, bought us a wood-burning stove, and set us up with tons of "presto" logs, which were ideal. I remember that wood-burning stove was irresistible for Andy and Jenny. Andy threw anything and everything into the fire to watch it burn. Dishtowels were one of his favorites. When Andy and Jenny tried to pull a burning towel out of the fire, it left burn holes in the carpet. I also recall some burn marks on a bare bottom when Andy tried to go behind the wood-burning stove when it was operating.

What I recall most is what a great mom Carla was when it came to raising the kids. She did not put up with much fussing or whining and I recall many times that she got down on the floor to be eye to eye with the kids to make her point. She went to every school function that they were involved in and made sure they were involved in all kinds of parades and functions during the summers. Andy was the biggest challenge Carla and I faced, and Carla was his biggest and best advocate in making sure he got the best possible opportunities in preschool and regular school. He was also her biggest concern when she knew she was going to die. She was the best mother for our kids that they could possibly have had and I'm sure they would agree, regardless of the rare pat on the backside.

By August 1975 we already had three children and by 1976 we were living in the Helena Valley in a mobile home on an acre of land, on Ferry Drive.

Les, I remember that land—you were in the wide-open spaces in the Helena Valley. It was beautiful. You could see the lights of Helena at night and there was nothing blocking your view in any direction. Really reminded me of that old Western you used to play as a kid, "Don't Fence Me In."

Yeah, great views, that's what it was like. Carl and Frances helped us a lot. He bought a 12 by 24-foot addition for our mobile home that added a lot of space. We paid him back. When we first moved out there, Carl always had horses. When it was winter and cold outside, the horses backed their butts up onto the warm trailer and took out windows. So that's when I had to get busy and put up a fence. So once they started busting the windows out I got a bunch of posts and 2 x 4s to fence the acre. I really needed to fence those horses out! I dug the north side by hand—over 200 feet—and after that, I rented a post-hole digger. I got black and blue from that darn post-hole digger—it kept hitting me in the side. So I taped a pillow to me that protected me from that gas-powered auger. Well, all it did was help me get black and blue more slowly. I finally asked somebody to help me, I don't remember who. Gee, that's only been thirty-five years ago, you think I could remember that stuff!

Life in the valley as far as I was concerned was a great place to raise kids. We couldn't keep clothes on the kids—they were always taking off their clothes! We went to the irrigation ditch as a family and had a picnic by the canal. We got into the water and swam against the current but stayed in one place. It was safe with adults there to keep an eye on the kids. At the same time Carl gave us an acre of ground, he also gave an acre to his daughter Georgia. Soon after we moved out there, maybe only after about a year, she built her house and moved out. That was nice for Carla to have her family nearby for a while and I know it was great for Georgia's son Ryan—he was at our house all the time playing with our kids. He was always in the mix. He and Adam are still close friends.

The first winter we were there—the winter of 1976-77—we got a huge amount of snow. The wind always blew from the north and because the trailer faced east and west, the snow piled up on the north side of the trailer to the point where a drift formed that was as high as the trailer. Yet right next to the trailer itself, a two-foot strip was bare ground. The drift was nine-feet high and as wide as the trailer was long. It tapered down to nothing after 100 to 150 feet. That was the only year that the snowdrift was as tall as the trailer. It was the darndest thing.

In the valley the kids were going to Jim Darcy Elementary School. The school was named after a Vietnam veteran who was killed in action in the 1960s. This was a great school for the kids because they always had so many activities. What impressed me was that Carla was involved with everything that the school did—classroom work and extracurricular activities.

I remember bringing Wayne, Rina, and Bethany as a baby to Darcy school functions. The kids had fun at the school—I particularly remember the Halloween parties. And if I recall they were not necessarily on Halloween so they could still go trick or treating.

Yeah, there were always functions that included all of the kids and their parents at Halloween, Christmas, Easter, and parties at other times, too. Carla always made sure that I went along—whether I wanted to or not. She was involved with all of the school functions. I was always glad that I went because I saw a lot of people who I knew from work and town, which surprised me. It always turned out to be a lot of fun, better than what I thought it was going to be. Carla always cooked food or treats for the school's activities and functions. She always thought it was important to be involved. I look back on Dad and he was not involved at all with our school activities. I remember Mom going to my parent-teacher conferences. Dad did go to parent-teacher conferences with Norm—because he always got into trouble. Norm said that eventually his teachers asked him to just ask Mom to go to his parent-teacher conferences because Dad was so intense and serious at the conferences it intimidated the teacher(s).

In the summer Carla enrolled the kids in activities. Swim lessons, stampede parade, and lots of other things. She kept them busy. Carla did art projects with them—always making something or building something. I was not always so involved with stuff going on with the kids because I was working and doing my own thing. Carla sewed all kinds of clothes for the kids, for the boys and Jenny, too. She often bought patterns. Halloween was always a big deal. She sewed costumes for the kids.

Carla worked hard at keeping the kids busy and entertained. She took them to a lot of Disney movies when they came out and to her favorite spot for ice cream and sodas. The ice cream parlor was always a favorite for the kids' birthdays. She took the kids to the Parrot, RB's Drive In, or Gerties—she went out of her way to take the kids to her favorite places. I think she made things fun for them. Even our brother Mark talked about how Carla took him down to RB's for a hamburger and Coke. He has great memories of her—she was like a big sister to him. When we first got married Mark was just a kid; he was only eleven years older than our son Adam.

My life with Carla when the kids were pretty young is what I have been talking about mostly. Life was always kind of hardscrabble when it came to having three kids and both of us having technical jobs that didn't pay much, but somehow we managed to do fun things with the kids.

One neat thing we did was go camping with the kids on the property on McClellen Creek that Carl owned. Every now and then, Frances wanted to go there too, so we barbecued hamburgers and hot dogs and shared a meal with her. Frances really liked that place. The family once owned a little cabin on the property, and when Carla and Georgia were little girls, they spent the weekends there with their grandparents. It was always a tradition to go there and camp on Memorial Day weekend. We pitched tents and had a lot of fun. It was a big party and oftentimes Carla's sister, Georgia, and her second husband, Dan, were there as well. Carla's brother, Jerry Heitzman, also came up too, driving here from Washington. Jerry came to Montana to live for a couple of years, but he could never find steady work so he ended up moving back to Washington.

Dan McGowan, Georgia's husband, had a horse when they were living in the valley. He kept his horse with Carl's horses so there was a group of eight or ten horses. It was nice when Georgia and Dan were married because they took care of the horses and I didn't have to take care of the dang things. Some horses, including Dan's, were "herd bound" and when the horses are separated from each other, they can kind of go crazy. One time Dan took his horse (a gelding) to the East Helena parade where Dan's horse was around different kinds of horses that it did not know—not the usual group on Ferry Drive. Dan's horse reared up and fell over backwards on top of Dan at the parade— apparently because it was homesick for its own group of horses. Dan had a broken leg in seven places. He was fortunate that his horse had not landed on his chest or head.

Another time Dan was around this same horse and he walked around the back of the horse. The crazy horse kicked Dan in the ass and sent him flying. Dan showed me a huge bruise on his backside and it was the shape of a horse's foot. Eventually, Dan gave that horse up.

CHAPTER TEN
REMEMBERING CARLA AND OUR CHILDREN

You know, if Carla and I were still married we would be going on forty-two years—seems crazy. It's tough to remember the nuances of the little things that went on. Carla made a big impression on all the kids—the way that she raised them. There were things that she let slide, but when it came to their behavior or good manners, there were lots of things that she wouldn't tolerate. She really made the kids toe the line especially in public. I let them get away with more stuff and she didn't let them whine or beg for things in public—that wasn't going to fly with her. Her second to the last resort was always a wooden spoon that she kept on top of the refrigerator. She would threaten to whack them with the wooden spoon if they got out of line. I know Adam got whacked once or twice. Jenny may have gotten threatened with a spoon maybe once, but I'm sure Andy went through several sets of spoons—he just didn't get it!

I have a lot of pride and admiration for Carla's mothering skills, which are particularly amazing because she wasn't raised by a mother. It is my understanding that her biological mother left when she was about six months old; I don't know if it's true or not. I've seen pictures of her mother, Pat, holding Carla when she was about six months old up on McDonald Pass so that must have been just before she took off. Jim was left with two baby girls and he wanted to find a mother for those girls. Over the next six years, or maybe more, he married two more women and things just didn't work out. Jim told me why he decided to remain single until the girls were raised and gone—a decision he kept as he was single for twenty-five years or more. Jim met a gal in Montana whom I shall refer to as Petulant. Jim and Petulant lived in a Los Angeles suburb when Jim worked as an engineer in the area. One day when he came home from work, there was a little girl sitting on the steps crying about how she had been a bad girl. She was so beat up that Jim didn't recognize his own daughter Carla. She was about five years old at that time. Jim told the story of taking Petulant down to the floor with his hands around her throat. He was going to kill her but he stopped himself. So that was the end of that marriage and he brought his girls home to Helena.

When it came time for Carla to be a mother, she read all the psychology books she could about parenting and she educated herself on the scholastic side of parenting. Carla was very protective. She was going to make damn sure that our kids were not beat on like she was. But that is not the way that you and I were raised. Being whacked on by Dad was commonplace for us. When that's the way you've been raised that's generally how you raise your own kids. I didn't know any different— so the very first time that I got pissed and I wanted to spank one of the kids, I was immediately confronted by Carla and she got right in my face and she told me that if I was going to beat on our kids she was going to take the kids and leave. That was that. There was no negotiating that point. I'm sure that brought up feelings in her of when she was a five-year-old girl getting beat on by her stepmother, and she was sure not going to let that happen to our kids.

That turned out to be a good philosophy. That doesn't mean that an occasional spoon wasn't applied to an ass—but there was not going to be any beating or jerking around of the children; that kind of stuff does real harm. Carla's form of discipline was geared toward the intellect and not the physical. She made the kids think about why what they were doing was wrong at the moment, always talking things out and talking things through. There was never any question in the kids' minds about why they were being punished. If I had my way, my shoe would be addressing their butts but I couldn't do that, she wouldn't let me.

In retrospect, Carla always had an extraordinary amount of patience that I didn't have. I don't know if that was instinctual or if she worked really hard at it. But it seemed like I had a much shorter fuse. I remember when we lived in the Helena Valley the water was so hard that it clogged the screens in the washing machine regularly. They were in a really tight spot behind the machine so I thought, "Why am I cleaning these screens? I should just take them out." Then I made the extremely intelligent decision to just take the screens off instead of cleaning them regularly. So one night we were watching TV and when I walked into the kitchen, there was water in the middle of the floor, so I started to mop it up. Then I walked into the bedroom next to the kitchen and there was also water there. The next bedroom and the bathroom were also full of water and I kept mopping. The water was coming from the washing machine, so I checked it over and over again and everything seemed to be working. We were doing laundry and everything seemed to be okay. So we go back to watching TV and about an hour later I went back into the kitchen and once again there was water going from the bathroom to the kitchen! This was happening weeks after I took the screens off so I didn't make the connection. At about this time I was starting to get pissed. After I cleaned everything up a second time, I went back to watch TV; I had to completely empty everything out of the bottom of the cabinets for each cleaning so I did this twice. I opened up the kitchen cabinets a third time and they were full of water again, so I grabbed the pots and pans on the bottom of the cabinets and I started flinging them around the kitchen. I was a raving mad man. I remember being so upset that I scared Carla and she said she was going to grab the kids and leave! I'm sure I apologized after I calmed down and she said she still loved me.

It finally dawned on me that it was me who caused the problem and it was the screens that stopped sand and dirt coming from the well. The sand ate up and destroyed the plastic valves so the valves attached to the hoses would not close. I had to buy new valves with screens, so from then on I just cleaned the screens. So never let your husband take those screens off—you will pay the price!

There was always stuff that was breaking and needed to be fixed at home, and we were in a position that if we didn't fix these things, they just didn't get fixed. Because back in those days we didn't have a spare nickel. When Carla and I were first married and when we were really poor, it seemed to me that Dad would gauge how we were doing financially, because every now and then he would ask me if he could borrow twenty dollars. Eventually, he bought us a Franklin stove and presto logs and kept us supplied with those things. He bought us 500 pounds of presto logs at a time. Every time he came out to visit he was packing food with him.

Les, I remember that about Dad, he was very generous.

Over time it seemed that Carla became fonder of Dad and they kind of teased each other. She wasn't at all intimidated by him. They had a pretty nice relationship and she was actually fond of him because he was so generous and she wasn't influenced by the past like we were. He *always* treated her with respect and didn't have any awful nicknames for her like he did his own daughters and sons. They had an adult relationship, not that of a father-daughter relationship. It took time because he was gruff and coarse and abrasive at times.

Carla liked most people; she always looked for the best in each person. She wasn't prone to gossiping. It was even difficult for her to discuss Georgia, who was completely different than her, or even be negative about her own mother who abandoned her. And speaking of her biological mother, Pat, we didn't even meet her until we had been married about five or six years. Out of the blue I get a call from Pat and she tells me that she and her husband, Bill, are going to be going through town on their motorcycle. So I told her, "Well, you are going to have to stop by and visit us." And then she tells me again that she and her husband Bill are going to be coming through town on his motorcycle and again I tell her, "You'll have to stop by and visit us on your way through town!" And then the third time that she said that she and Bill are going to be coming through town on his motorcycle, it finally dawns on me that she is asking to stay with us. So I said, "You can come and stay with us," and she said "Whew! Thank you, Les!" Pat slowly came back into Carla's life and mine as well. I think Carla felt closer to her as time went on and found peace with her mother.

So there is a pattern here that is emerging—it takes me three times to figure out what is going on, like washing machine valves and mothers-in-law. I don't catch on the first two times but by the third time I finally get it.

CHAPTER ELEVEN

THE SPECIAL WEEK

I have a very special memory of Carla and me. One summer all of the kids went to different camps during the same week, and Carla and I got a taste of what it would be like for us to be empty nesters. We were so consumed with the responsibility of our kids that it was almost shocking to have all of them gone at the same time—we didn't know how to act. It was almost like going back to the time when all we had was each other. It was a nice little break. It was our first vacation away from the kids. It was fun and great. We went to the movies and out to dinner.

We talked about what it would be like when our kids were grown. I think we were still working but we had freedom; it was something that we hadn't had for at least ten years of raising kids.

CHAPTER TWELVE
"KNOCKING ON HEAVEN'S DOOR"

I know that this is the time to start talking about when Carla was diagnosed with cancer. There was a time when she started throwing up on a daily basis and after a short time of this happening, she went to her doctor, a general practitioner, at least three times, maybe more, over three months. He kept coming up with things that her sickness could be—maybe gall bladder, etc. After the third time that she went back to him, the doctor finally realized that it was a bigger problem than he could deal with and he referred her to Dr. Cade, an internist. We just didn't have any idea it was so serious—I thought it was some type of intestinal infection.

Carla went to see Dr. Cade and he made the diagnosis within twenty-four hours after her first visit. He called her in to see him in his office. He gave Carla the news that she had terminal cancer and had twelve to eighteen months to live. He was the first doctor to tell her that she was going to die and that what she needed to do was to get in touch with an oncologist right away. This was over twenty-five years ago. At that time we had no cancer treatment center in town. If you had cancer you had the choice of going to Missoula, Great Falls, or Butte. We picked Butte because it was the closet to Helena. I'm sure Doctor Cade forwarded all of her test results to Butte.

Prior to going to Butte, of course, Carla had to break the news to her family. She told me first. We went into the bedroom and we closed the door. She was very brave and when she told me, I just couldn't believe the words; she told me straight up that she had terminal cancer and had twelve to eighteen months to live. After she told me I think that my body went into shock; I was freezing cold for about three days and no matter how much I turned up the heat, I was freezing cold. I don't recall how she broke it to the kids; I think we gathered as a group and we broke the news together, but maybe Carla talked to them one at a time; I cannot remember all of the details because I think I was in shock. Carla was calling the shots on how everything was happening and who she talked to after her diagnosis. After the initial shock started to wear off, I experienced an upwelling of anger inside me that seemed like it was all consuming for a long time.

What I do recall about going to Butte that impressed me was the attitude that the cancer staff had toward the cancer patient. Up until that time, whenever I went into a doctor's office, I felt like I was at the mercy of the doctor and that I had to do whatever the doctor said. The experience at the Butte Cancer Center was totally different. The patient called the shots and was in control of the situation. That doesn't mean that we didn't have to face the brutal truth. The oncologist told Carla that she needed to get her affairs in order because "you are going to die." Twenty-five years ago, he said that 80 percent of cancers that they deal with their hands are tied and there is nothing they can do and 20 percent of cancers they can deal with and help the patient. I think now those numbers are reversed. Carla was diagnosed with adenocarcinoma; they tried to find where it started through a lot of testing. Everywhere they looked they found cancer. It was in her liver, lungs, and all of her organs. My personal feeling is that the cancer started in her ovaries or pancreas. The doctor said that this type of cancer hits 1 in 40,000 people and typically is found in men over sixty years old.

We discussed chemotherapy; the oncologist made it clear that chemotherapy would not change the outcome of the disease. When you've just turned thirty-six and you've been given a death sentence, you still have hope that chemotherapy may extend your life a little bit. So we had the hope that the chemotherapy would buy her a little more time. She was young and had been healthy and vibrant her entire life so we just couldn't throw out hope. So it was with hope that she might gain a little more time that Carla agreed to do the chemo. In retrospect I don't know that the chemo added any time to her life and it did not improve the quality of her life. That is my personal opinion. She went through two rounds of it, and when it came to the third round of it she said that's enough—because it just made her feel so bad.

After the second round of chemotherapy was finished, we had the opportunity to go to Puerto Vallarta, Mexico, with our good friends Greg and Robin. We had a really, really good time. Carla wanted to go parasailing out over the ocean, so the four of us got on a boat and went. Carla was first and she was really excited and brave. She stood on a harness that was tied to a huge parachute. When she was all buckled in, two or three guys hung onto the chute. It was very windy and if they let go she would go up immediately. After the boat and parachute were ready the men let go of the chute and Carla flew straight up into the air around 200 feet. The boat took us out over the ocean for about twenty minutes. Carla was reluctant to come down from flying through the air on the parasail; the guys on the boat kept trying to get her to pull on the ropes so she could begin lowering herself onto the boat. Finally, Carla relented and manipulated her ropes to begin her descent back toward the earth. She loved flying like a free bird.

Unbeknownst to me, coworkers from the City of Helena raised money for our family during a fundraiser. One day I went to work and my boss handed me a check for $3,500 and he said it was for me but it was not to pay bills. So that got me thinking about making a big trip. I used this money to fund a good portion of a trip all around the country in our camper with the kids, their cousin Ryan Drake and Benji (our dog). We covered about 9,000 miles.

I wanted to see as many of our relatives as possible. So we started in Salt Lake City, Utah, where Diane and Mike were living and then we went to Marysville, California, to see Aunt Marlene and Aunt Evelyn. I remember poor Benji had to stay outside because the people we were visiting did not allow him in the house because Benji was just covered with fleas; we had to get a lot of medicine for him to get rid of them.

Then we traveled to Vallejo, California, to see Uncle Raymond, and then we went down to San Diego to visit the zoo and Sea World. We managed to stay at KOAs for most of the trip. I remember one night we stayed in El Centro, California—below sea level—and it was so hot that the boys elected to sleep outside. In the morning they were covered with 300 to 400 mosquito bites. They were miserable.

From San Diego we followed US Highway 10 and went all the way across the country toward Florida. We stopped in Houston, and the boys, including Ryan Drake, and I went to a professional baseball game between the Astros and the Philadelphia Phillies. Carla and Jenny went to the mall, shopping. I spent under $20 for tickets for four of us to get into the ball game. But to buy a hotdog and a Coke cost over $50 for the four of us, including one beer for me! Also on this trip we stayed in New Orleans where we were at an absolutely beautiful KOA; it was lush and green and really beautiful. The kids were good and they had fun; I'm sure it was memorable for each of them.

Les, that was such a special time for all of you.

Yes it was. We finally made it to Florida and we went to Disney World for three days. This was in August and during the entire trip the outside temperature reached 110 degrees F. (But that's why it was so great watching baseball in the Astrodome, the temperature was 72 degrees F.) I think the kids really enjoyed Disney World, it was such a great place for them. Carla felt as good as she could feel; she wasn't on chemo. At Disney World she stood in line with the kids, got them on rides but was too frail to go on any of them. At Epcot Center she did go on one ride (a ride where the room moved) because she could sit. Carla spent a lot of time sleeping. Any chance she had to sit she fell asleep, especially if it was cool. She took all kinds of medications, some of them for pain. On a good day she threw up only once, on bad days she threw up eight to ten times. Most of the days were good days.

In Florida, we were at a KOA in Kissimmee and big, English-style double-decker buses stopped by regularly and took people to Disney World. Once we were there we didn't have to drive anywhere because the buses took us back to the KOA whenever we wanted. On the third day I discovered that I had left the key on in the ignition of the truck, which completely drained the battery. So Carla and the kids went to Disney World and I had to stay with the truck; I had to go find a battery charger. I needed to walk five miles to get to a Walmart. It was brutally hot. When I crossed bridges over waterways I saw alligators. That was interesting. I finally found Walmart, the first one I had ever seen in my life, and by golly, they had a battery charger! So I bought it and I walked the five miles back to camp. I got back to the campground so I could hook up the battery charger. Soon after, I drank two cold beers and they were the best beers I'd ever had in my life!

The following day, we drove up to Glennville, Georgia, and spent a few days with Uncle Gail, and what a respite that was. He took us in and treated us great. It was about that time that I was running out of cash, so Uncle Gail gave me two or three credit cards and I used them for gas to get us home. When I got home I wrote a check to cover everything and sent him back his credit cards.

Les, I really have great memories of Uncle Gail. He was such a good man—a sweetheart and a kind and gentle person.

On our way home we went to DeWitt, Iowa, to see Carla's relatives and her Aunt Evelyn was there; she was Carla's grandmother Frances' sister. Her Aunt Evelyn and Uncle Nels also treated us wonderfully and showed us the sites all around DeWitt. We went to a graveyard on the Harrington side and one of the birthdays on the headstones went back to 1806. They also showed us where Frances and her husband, George, had lived and ran a meat market. Carla was able to see what her grandmother's life was like before she moved out to Montana.

Our next stop was to see Norm, who lived in Evergreen just outside Denver. At that time Mom and Aunt Bernadine were visiting at Norm's home. On our way home we picked up Mom and Aunt Bernadine and drove them back to Helena with us.

Wow! The whole trip was 9,000 miles and it cost $900 in gas! I was pretty bummed out about the price of gas—it was a dollar a gallon and it just seemed outrageous!

Wow Les, what an amazing journey you took with Carla, Adam, Andy,

Jenny, Ryan, and Benji. I'm sure that was a special time for Mom and Aunt Bernadine spending quality time with all of you. I know this was a very, very sad time but you and Carla had so much courage and you made this a wonderful time, packing in a lifetime of precious memories for you and your children.

Now it's the summer of 1987 and it probably wasn't very long after we got back after that trip that Carla got steadily worse. Eventually she could no longer drive because of the drugs, and the cancer was beginning to take its toll. It was during the trip that she decided that there was going to be no more chemo. The chemo was really, really hard on her and made her sick—the cancer made her sick and that was more than just throwing up—but the chemo on top of that made her really miserable. I'm not sure what the time frame was—but tumors were beginning to take over her body.

When we got home from our trip Carla and I started talking about getting hospice to help us. This is when your nursing classmate, Chris Anderson, started to come over and help. Carla was getting to the point where she needed a lot of help with everything. She stayed independent as long as possible, but because of the pain medications and drugs that she was taking she was not able to function normally. She began to lose her train of thought and the ability to follow through with a conversation.

Toward the end of her life, Carla flew down to Sedona, Arizona, to spend time with her grandmother; at that time she still had the wherewithal to catch her flights. Carla recorded Frances telling some stories about when she was young so our kids could hear some of the family stories. Carla wanted to pass on some family continuity.

After she returned from Arizona, Carla started to really take a serious turn for the worse; she was retaining a lot of fluid and became very distended because of the cancer in her liver. Her ability to function became less and less, and she spent more and more time sleeping. Eventually, she stopped talking and moving altogether, and at that point she needed twenty-four-hour care. At that time I went to my boss and told him I was going home and not coming back to work until Carla was gone. These were the last two weeks of her life.

During these last two weeks she never spoke and even stopped blinking. I got prescription eye drops for Carla and put them in her eyes. Because of severe edema in her legs and feet, she also wore support stockings that were very difficult for us to put on her. There was a point during those two weeks that she was just really agitated, so I just guessed at what she wanted me to do. I moved her from the bed to the couch to the chair to the bed and finally, about 4:00 A.M., I put her in bed and laid down beside her. I was just exhausted. The next thing I knew I heard the doorbell ringing, ringing, ringing. I woke up and Carla was gone; she was not in the bed next to me. I got up and ran to the front door and there she was, standing on the front porch, totally naked. She was very scared and her eyes were wide open. She had somehow gotten up, undressed herself, and went outside. This was January in Montana. So I brought her in, put her in the waterbed, and warmed her up. I can only speculate as to what she was thinking.

The next day I called up her regular doctor and her oncologist in Butte. One of the doctors prescribed Haldol for her and I think that helped keep her from being so agitated. At this point I don't think any drugs had much effect, including suppositories. Her ability to take in water or any kind of food was so minimal. She was on very high doses of pure liquid morphine for pain and I realized that I was giving her too much. I didn't realize how much I was giving her, I had misread the dosage label. So I called her doctor and told him, "I did a terrible thing. I was supposed to be giving Carla 0.1 ml of morphine and I have been giving her 1.0 ml of morphine. Ten times the dose." The doctor said, "Les, don't feel bad for one second. You have done her a favor by not extending her life." He also said that if I have shortened her life at all I was doing her a favor. He did not tell me to lower her dose or do anything differently.

It was then I decided I was not going to let her go into a hospital and let them plug her into all kinds of machines to extend her life. I was not going to let that happen. After that there were no more psychotic episodes. I continued to take care of her constantly and the hospice nurses were coming over all of the time. They applied a product called New-Skin to help with the bedsores that she was beginning to develop. Every so often I carried her into the bathroom to see if she could go. And we would carry her into the bathtub to give her baths every day. Her movement was pretty limited by this time. Her last few days she was totally bedridden.

During the last few weeks I got a second wind and realized I could take care of her. It was probably because of all of the help that we received from family and friends. Georgia was there, Robin, Carla's very close friend, was there, and you were there, Jeannette. People were obviously helping make meals for the kids; Adam spent a lot of time with friends—staying at their houses. Andy and Jennifer stuck around the house for the most part.

On the night that Carla passed away Adam was with his buddy Derrick—everyone knew that Carla was going to die—we just didn't know when. Just when I knew that it was very close at hand Dan McGowan came over and dragged me out of the house and said, "We are gonna go get a beer." He dragged me down to the Suds Hut and I remember drinking that beer down fast because I wanted to get back home. I said, "Dan, I need to get back home," so he took me back home.

When I walked in the door Robin walked up to me and said, "Carla wants you, she's dying." So I went to the bedroom door where several people were standing. I walked into the bedroom and closed the door. I kneeled on the floor next to Carla and started talking to her. I told her how much I loved her and what an honor it was to have met her, married her, and had kids with her. She turned over on her side, lifted herself up on her elbow, and put her face right next to mine. There were tears coming down her eyes. She didn't speak because she couldn't speak. But she was saying goodbye. Then she laid back down and drew her last breath, and then, she died.

*

That was the most powerful, emotional thing that I had ever been through. I thought Dad's death was a powerful thing and it was, but it just didn't compare to losing Carla. Because it was such an emotional, powerful thing, I made it the most important thing in my life. It wasn't until a couple of decades passed that I was able to have a different perspective. It finally dawned on me, twenty years later, that Carla's passing was not the most important thing that ever happened to me—it was just the saddest thing that ever happened. Meeting Carla was more important than her dying, falling in love with her was more important than her dying, having our children was more important than her dying, and even going through her illness was more important than her dying. Her death did not define her; her life defined her. It was so difficult for me to realize this, but the passage of time brings a different perspective to her life. Everything about her was more important than the end of her life.

I have a memory of you that took place several months after Carla passed. Moonshine was playing at the Staggering Ox. You were front and center on stage. The bar was packed, alcohol was flowing freely, beer and whiskey, and the smoke was thick. Suddenly you started singing this song in your clear, beautiful voice:

"Silver Wings"
By Merle Haggard, 1969

"Silver wings shining in the sunlight
roaring engines headed somewhere in flight
they're taking you away, leaving me lonely
Silver wings slowly fading out of sight

Don't leave me I cry
don't take that airplane ride
but you locked me out of your mind
and left me standing here behind

Silver wings shining in the sunlight
roaring engines headed somewhere in flight
they're taking you away, leaving me lonely
Silver wings slowly fading out of sight

Don't leave me I cry
don't take that airplane ride
but you locked me out of your mind
and left me standing here behind

Silver wings shining in the sunlight
roaring engines headed somewhere in flight
they're taking you away, leaving me lonely
Silver wings slowly fading out of sight"

At that moment there was no one else there. You looked above the faces and the heads of the crowd and saw no one. It was just you and Carla.

Carla and I talked about you and I knew how much she loved you. There is a song that keeps coming to mind as I am writing this memoir with you. I cannot explain it—perhaps she has found a way to reach me and has put it into my mind. All I can say is the song won't leave. I really believe in my heart that if she were here she would want you to hear these words. This would be Carla's song to you.

"You're The Best Thing That Ever Happened To Me"
By Jim Weatherly, 1973

"I've had my share of life's ups and downs
But fate has been kind, the downs have been few
I guess you could say that I've been lucky
Well, I guess you could say that it's all because of you

If anyone should ever write my life story
For whatever reason there might be
Ooh, you'll be there between each line of pain and glory
'cause you're the best thing that ever happened to me

Oh, there have been times when times were hard
But always somehow I made it, I made it through
'cause for every moment that I've spent hurting
There was a moment that I spent, oh, just loving you

If anyone should ever write my life story
For whatever reason there might be
Ooh, you'll be there between each line of pain and glory
'cause you're the best thing that ever happened to me
Oh, you're the best thing that ever happened to me
I know you're the best thing, oh, that ever happened to me."

CHAPTER THIRTEEN
LIFE ALONE AS A SINGLE PARENT

A very important thing happened to me when Carla was sick. The Public Works Director asked City of Helena employees to collectively donate a month's worth of sick leave time for me to use after Carla passed away. My fellow employees did this as I was completely out of sick leave and vacation days. It was the first time in the history of Helena that city employees were allowed to donate their sick leave time to each other. I had one month alone with my children as we began our new journey together without their mother and my love.

We were all in shock after Carla's death so the kids and I went to grief therapy classes. I went to my doctor and he signed a form so that the insurance company would pay for the counseling. I think the therapy classes were through St. Peter's Hospital. When I was going to a therapy class there were about eight women; the youngest was about fifteen years older than me and the oldest was about eighty years old. I was the only man and only thirty-six years old. I didn't particularly want to go but thought if I was going to make the kids go then there was no way I could back out of the sessions myself. At first it was kind of strange, you know, opening up in front of all of the women, but it didn't take me long to realize that they were feeling the exact kind of feelings that I was. Carla and I had been together for about twenty years and married for about seventeen of those years; some of those gals had been married for over fifty years. Their grief was every bit as great as mine. At the same time we formed a bond from our common experience. They were very kind and gentle to me. The women were so open about their personal feelings and thoughts, helping me do the same. To this day, whenever I run into some of these gals, even twenty-five years later, they still come up to me and give me hug and ask how I'm doing. They have a genuine concern for my welfare. I still run into some of the younger women who were in the group.

I don't think the kids got that much out of the grief therapy sessions. They were talking to adults and not other children. I remember talking to Jenny about it and don't think it was some type of transcendental type of experience; it was just some other goddamn thing that Dad made them do.

One thing that I do recall is kind of being pissed about life. I just felt it was so unfair that Carla was taken. I remember that Rick was working with me at the City and he did his best to console me with comforting words. I feel bad about rebuffing his attempts to console me but I think I was inconsolable. I remember being pissed for so long that I just thought I would be this angry for the rest of my life and that's just the way it was. Eventually, that feeling started to subside.

After Carla died, one of the first things I did was go to the Social Security office and apply for survivor benefits for the kids. I started getting money from Social Security—something like $200 per child per month. The benefits stopped when the kids turned eighteen years old. As it turned out, I received approximately $20,000 for the kids, and I tell you that was a terrific help. I even wrote a letter to the Social Security Administration and thanked them for all of the help over the years until each of my children reached the age of eighteen. I was grateful. It didn't make up for what Carla was bringing home but it certainly helped.

On Memorial Day that year, the first time since Carla's funeral, the kids and I put flowers on her grave. I was really worried about the kids—how they would do and everything. My plan was to be strong for the kids but I was just overwhelmed with grief and I just dropped to my knees. Adam, Andy, and Jenny stood around me and put their hands on me. They were comforting me and it was just the opposite of what I thought would happen that day. I was so shocked about how powerful those emotions were, four months after the fact. It shouldn't have surprised me but it did.

It took me back to a time that was about six months after Dad had died. I remembered telling Carla that Dad's death didn't have much effect on me and Carla looked at me and said, "Are you crazy?!" She could see it but I couldn't. About that time a song came out by Dan Fogelberg called "The Leader of the Band," When I heard it I just wept really hard. Some of the words were, "I don't think I told you I loved you near enough," and that song made me think of Dad and that I didn't remember ever telling him that I loved him.

I don't remember Dad being an emotional person who freely expressed his feelings. I have a few memories of talking to him about his feelings or being really upset about something but those conversations were few and far between.

In retrospect I shouldn't have been so surprised that going to Carla's grave would be so difficult.

Your children were really wonderful.

Yeah, and I know it was tough on them.

CHAPTER FOURTEEN
ADAM

When Adam was seventeen he signed up for the military—I think he was a junior, going into his senior year of high school. At seventeen kids can sign up with their parents' permission. So one day in the spring, when it was toward the end of Adam's junior year, I came home from work and there were two Army recruiting officers in my living room.

They presented me with papers to sign giving my permission for Adam to commit himself to join the Army after he graduated from high school. The officers gave a brief explanation as to why they were there and then I asked them, "Did Adam tell you that his mother just died?" And they said, "No sir." I told them that Adam had had an awful lot of change in his life recently and I wanted him to be able to deal with that before making any more huge changes in his life, so I wasn't signing anything. They didn't argue, they just said ok and left. The officers were very polite; they weren't salesmen, so that was it. If truth be told it was probably me that didn't want more change rather than Adam not being ready for change. Adam and I didn't even have a chance to talk about it before the officers came to the house and I had to make a decision really fast. Adam was really angry for about twenty-four hours. Eventually, he was really happy that he wasn't signed up to go into the military immediately after high school graduation.

During the first summer after the kids' mom died, I wanted to do something different for them so they had good memories other than of their mom dying. So I sent Adam, Andy, and Jenny on a monthlong trip. They flew to Nashville first to see their Aunt Diane and family, then to Phoenix to see their Uncle Norm, and eventually to Sacramento to see you, Jeannette, and your family. During that summer, 1988, our air quality in Helena was horrible because Yellowstone National Park and forests in the state were burning up. We experienced severe air inversions and during the day the sun was just a red ball.

I remember not being able to pay bills on time—maybe this was when Adam went off to college two years after Carla passed. The only way I could afford to pay Montana State University for his education was to work out some kind of deal with the university. I had to pay them $500 a month and that was just a shit load of money for me at the time. Adam's first choice for college was the University of the Pacific in California; he wanted to study International Business, and at that time, the school tuition there was around $20,000 a year. It was just economically unfeasible. The best that I could do for him was send him to school in Bozeman. After two years Adam wanted to move to Boise, Idaho, to attend Boise State and I wasn't supportive of that idea. He had friends who moved from Bozeman to Boise and he wanted to follow them. I tried to be very persuasive with Adam and control him by telling him I would continue to help him if he stayed at MSU but I would not help him if he moved to Idaho. I thought he would stay because he didn't have any choice. I thought wrong.

Adam moved to Idaho anyway. He is a lot like Norm, very strong-willed and independent. If his "old man's" plan didn't coincide with his, too damn bad! But I always knew that Adam was going to be able to take care of himself whatever path he chose because he was smart and intelligent and savvy about getting by. Very, very intelligent.

I was falling behind in paying my bills more and more until it finally got to the point that bills didn't mean much until they were accompanied by a pink slip. That was hard. I experienced a tremendous financial burden just paying for Adam's college and supporting my three kids as a single dad. But I was bound and determined to see it through.

Adam started working in Boise and found his own path. He

attended Boise State University for one year, continuing his study of International Business. Because he was a junior he could get all of the financing that he needed from student loans. I know that for him, it made all the difference in the world to be a junior.

After that year Adam quit school and I believe he worked various jobs for the next four years. He tried different things he thought he might like to pursue. Adam worked as a waiter at several establishments, including the Charter House, an upscale restaurant. In order to become a full-fledged waiter he needed to apprentice there with no pay for one year. He did that. He stuck it out and he became a full-fledged waiter after one year. After he busted his ass waiting on rude people who weren't half as smart as he was, with a smile, he decided that that was not what he wanted to do for the rest of his life. So he went back to school to pursue a degree in computer science, starting once again as a freshman in college. Technically, he wasn't a freshman, he was a senior! He qualified for school loans to finish his degree in computer science. So I think it was around 2000 that Adam graduated from Boise State University with his degree in computer science. Adam now works as a software engineer and fortunately, he has been very successful in this profession. Without a doubt Adam made the best choice of a career for himself—it fits him to a "T." He really turned out great, but he had to do it his way. Adam needed to walk his own path.

CHAPTER FIFTEEN

ANDY

Andy was thirteen and in the sixth grade when his Mom died. With the severe hearing loss that he suffered, he was only able to get by in elementary school; he had one teacher and one resource teacher, and between the two of them they were able to help him just scrape by with Cs and Ds. Andy was Carla's primary concern when she was sick and dying—she was worried about Andy because she didn't know how he would do without her. He was her biggest worry as far as the future. She knew that Adam and Jenny would be okay, but she was the personal protector of Andy and she just didn't know how he was going to make it. That really concerned her.

Andy finished the sixth grade after his mom passed away. The next year he started seventh grade, and instead of one teacher and one resource teacher he had six or seven teachers and one resource teacher. His grades went from Cs to Fs. His teachers called me at work regularly and talked to me about him. They said things like, "Why isn't he like his sister?" and "Andy is not doing this and he is not doing that . . . " I was at my wits end when a coworker asked me if I ever considered sending Andy to the Montana School for the Deaf and Blind (MSDB). Andy has a profound hearing loss on his left side and can hear only about 50 percent of sounds on the right side. His audiologist told me that what Andy hears without any type of hearing aids can be compared to tightly cupping both hands over the ears of a person who has no hearing loss. My coworker's children were involved with the Lion's swim club and one of the parents was the head administrator for the Special Education Department of the school district in Helena. Somehow my boss got wind of that—he was married to a teacher and somehow set up a time for me to meet with the administrator of the school. This was at the May Butler School. At that time it was the administration building for the school district. I walked up to the director of the Special Education Department and asked her point blank, "Is the Montana School for the Deaf and Blind a possibility for my son?" She replied, "Well, yes!"

So the staff at the elementary school where my son had attended school all these years had known about my son yet no one had ever mentioned the MSDB before. It's my belief that the reason it was never mentioned was because the money to pay for it would come out of the Helena School District budget. The school district administrators and teachers chose to watch him struggle to barely scrape by the entire time he was in elementary school instead of referring him to MSDB. After Andy started middle school it became obvious that he would not be able to make it because he was getting straight Fs.

The failing grades came before anybody knew he had Asperger's Syndrome. Only our immediate family knew that he had more challenges than a severe hearing loss. When I pressed the issue the school district officials finally conceded and allowed him to go to the MSDB on their dime. It was after the start of the school year and probably pretty close to the end of the first semester that arrangements were made for him to go to the MSDB in Great Falls, Montana. Andy was really upset and didn't want to go or leave home, but at that time I called the shots for him in order to give him a better education. This was still really close to the time Andy lost his mom.

Andy now had to live in a different town and could only come home on weekends. When the roads got really bad I could typically only bring him home every other weekend. Eventually, I brought him home every other weekend and that schedule lasted for five years. Andy, of course, came home every year on the anniversary of his mom's passing. He thought of everything he could so that he could come home. Sometimes when the roads were bad, I had him ride the bus and that was safer. I always traveled to Great Falls for his parent-teacher conferences.

Surprisingly, Andy always got As and Bs even though he professed to hate the school. He had to learn a second language at his new school—American Sign Language. Some of the best teachers at the school for the deaf and blind were deaf and could not speak. It was amazing and wonderful that Andy was put in a position to succeed academically for the first time in his life. There were times when he struggled there but that was when they mainstreamed him in the Great Falls public school's regular classes, beginning first in middle school and eventually into a high school setting. To accommodate the public school setting, the MSDB sent someone along with him to help him understand what was being said and I believe they used sign language.

The entire time he attended the MSDB he was not diagnosed with Asperger's Syndrome. The teachers tried very hard to socialize him, but they were not successful. Initially, he roomed with students who were deaf but because of his inability to socialize, they could not get along with him. There was one incident when a student put Andy's hand on a hot plate and burned him. Maybe the student got really angry about something that Andy did. I think the school tried to place several different deaf students as Andy's roommates but it never panned out. School administrators probably thought that if he can't get along with a deaf student that they'd try to pair him with a blind student. Andy thought it would be funny to put stuff on the floor in front of the blind kids and watch them fall because he loves slapstick. So he did. The experiment with a blind roommate ended when the roommate found Andy with his cane. The blind student went after Andy and hit him repeatedly with his cane and then picked Andy up and put him on his shoulder, swinging him around, bashing Andy's head against walls and doors and any other hard surface he could find. So Andy did a good job of pissing off the deaf students as well as the blind students! Only after that incident did the school realize that Andy needed his own room. From that time on, for more than four years at the MSDB, he had his own room. Andy has always been an easy target for bullies, so it was a very good decision.

The MSDB gets a lot of funding from the legislature. They have excellent programs for extracurricular activities and for traveling. Andy traveled with teachers and students and they went on great trips all over the country, including Washington, D.C. There, he personally met Senator Max Baucus, Conrad Burns, and other Montana politicians.

One time there was a huge storm that paralyzed the East Coast; Andy's class was supposed to fly to the East Coast but the flight was cancelled due to poor weather conditions. So that weekend, I brought Andy home. About 5:00 A.M. I got a call that the flight was still on and I needed to get him to the Great Falls airport by 7:00 A.M. Andy and I got up and got dressed and packed some stuff and threw it in the car and I drove about 100 miles per hour. I flew right by a highway patrolman and I immediately pulled over and he pulled in behind me. He got out of his car and walked up to me and said, "Did you need to talk to me?" So I told him that I was taking my son to the airport and that he was a student at the MSDB and he needed to be on the plane by 7:00 A.M. I told him I was going to be speeding and he just said, "Drive carefully," and I continued to drive 100 miles per hour all the way there. I felt like I had the patrolman's blessing. I got him to the airport with only ten minutes to spare. I drove my old Buick with a 403 cubic-inch engine—we affectionately called it the "banana boat." I think Andy took a trip south to Florida, too, and maybe to Disney World. I believe he also went to New York City. There was another great trip where the school took students to Minneapolis and St. Paul, Minnesota. In St. Paul there is a technical school for the deaf and blind. It is one of the premier schools in the entire country that is geared for individuals who are deaf and blind or both. I think it is called the St. Paul Technical Institute. The MSDB took all of the junior and senior students to St. Paul every year. The MSDB often had great opportunities for the students and they paid for everything that the students needed: transportation, hotels, meals, and sightseeing! There were also countless field trips in and around Great Falls. It was a great school and a wonderful opportunity for Andy. Yet Andy insisted on coming home at least every other weekend; he just never felt at home there.

Andy always felt that he didn't belong at the MSDB. Even though he was able to get good grades, he never felt like he should have been placed there. In my mind Andy never made the connection that he was totally failing here yet able to succeed there. He didn't see the difference between failure and success. To this day, I think that he believes I did the wrong thing for him. Regardless of how he feels, I did what I had to do. I want people to understand that it was my decision along with educational experts that Andy attend the MSDB. I had to make the decision after his mom had passed away.

I had just started dating Sue when it was time for Andy to graduate. Sue, her son, Bill, and Jenny all came to his graduation. The ceremony was very, very nice with lots of people using American Sign Language. The graduating class performed all kinds of songs using sign. However, even when we were coming home after his beautiful graduation, Andy told me that the last five years at the school was the biggest waste of time that he had ever experienced during his whole life. I tried to explain to him that he went from a school where he was completely failing to a school where he was successful and got all As and Bs. It didn't make a bit of difference to him, he still said it was a complete waste of his time.

After Andy graduated, the school sent him a large box containing all of his education files from preschool through twelfth grade. He promptly threw all of those records away. When I asked him why he did that he simply said, "I didn't want that." I was so disappointed. Why didn't they send them to me? I would have kept them. To me, those records were very valuable. It just didn't matter to him that he received an education.

One of the classes that Andy took at the school in Great Falls was so critical because it taught him skills to help him live independently: budgeting, personal finance, how to handle bills, how to cook and shop. Once he got out of school, Andy did have connections to places in Helena, but when he first got home he did not think he really needed to do anything. I forced him to get a job and eventually he attended the Helena Vocational Technical Center to learn carpentry skills such as cabinet making. He had all kinds of tools and I made sure that Andy sat at the front of his classes and that he had special hearing equipment so that he could hear the sounds of all of the tools as well as his teachers.

After attending the Vo-Tech school Andy got a job at Helena Industries. I was able to talk to his caseworkers and the people at Helena Industries because Andy signed a consent form giving me permission. We worked very hard to keep Andy motivated and for him to get to work on time. The head guy at Helena Industries, Ken, had no arms; he had been in a severe farming accident as a kid. Ken worked with Andy for at least two years and is the key to further understanding what was really happening with Andy and had been occurring his whole life. Ken found it difficult to get Andy to come to work on time. Once he got there, though, Andy worked hard and was very safety conscious, but he was never on time.

Ken said to me early on, "We're going to get to the bottom of this. We are going to help Andy." He set up an appointment with a psychologist named Greg Burns. Dr. Burns met with Andy and talked to him for about thirty minutes. Then the doctor brought in Jenny and myself. Dr. Burns talked to us for hours! I remember the last thing I said to him was, "I can't pigeonhole this kid. He reads extremely well, he's articulate but he just doesn't have any friends." Dr. Burns said, "Don't worry about that—that's my job." Very soon he came up with his diagnosis of Asperger's Syndrome.

With this diagnosis everything changed. The Social Security Administration said he was eligible for benefits and with Social Security came Medicaid. Both of these benefits took the financial burden off my shoulders. Andy was twenty-five years old when he was diagnosed; he continued to work at Helena Industries until he was twenty-eight years old. I tried so hard to get him to go to work every day, causing so much friction between us that all he wanted to do was physically fight me. I couldn't take the stress anymore so I went to his supervisor and his case workers and I told them that I was stepping back. If they had to fire him, go ahead and do it. I wasn't going to fight Andy and I wasn't going to fight them anymore. I asked them that if they fired Andy if they could please not do anything to affect his Social Security benefits. Helena Industries held that over his head for years by saying that if he did not go to work they would stop his benefits.

None of us could come up with a way to make Andy come to work at the same time every day. Sometimes he went to work at 9:00 or 10:00 A.M., noon, or 1 P.M. A person cannot just go to work whenever they feel like it! Helena Industries assured me they would not do anything to affect his Social Security benefits, and they didn't. You know, they were weary of the battle too. Nothing worked. When he was twenty-eight years old it dawned on me that I couldn't fix him, I couldn't change him, and the only recourse that I had, and ever had, was to accept him for who he was. He hadn't changed one bit from the day he was born, and I had spent twenty-eight years trying to fix him and change him and I couldn't do it. The only thing that had changed is now there was a name to the condition that described him. I realized that the only thing that could change was me. Andy didn't have the ability to change but I did. Ever since I stopped trying to change him, our personal relationship has become much better—our bond is more like my bond with my other two children. That doesn't mean that he still doesn't piss me off sometimes, but there is a greater understanding on my part. He won't change, and I'm the one that has to deal with it, not him.

To this day, Andy believes that he was misdiagnosed, that he doesn't have Asperger's, and that there is nothing wrong with him. Maybe the rest of the world is a little goofy, but he is not. I simply explained to him, "Thank God for that misdiagnosis because it pays for your living and your health care." He has a minimal standard of living but he has the Cadillac of health care benefits.

Ninety nine out of one hundred times I am very patient with him even though he can still push my buttons. One out of one hundred times I still fail miserably, as I can still get really upset with him. The truth is that in my lifetime, Andy has been my greatest teacher of patience.

I think of it as if we are looking through the fog—trying to see the light. We are just waiting for the fog to lift so that we can see clearly.

Surely as humans we are great at labeling everything—even the degrees of autism.

But do we really understand it? I think not; our knowledge base is only a glimpse. You once told me that the only thing we truly need when spending time with or living with someone who has autism is patience and caring.

I hope this verse will bring comfort to you and for those with autism as well as for the people who love them.

1 Corinthians 13:12
King James Version

For now we see through a glass,
darkly; but then face to face: now I
know in part; but then shall I know
even also as I am known.

CHAPTER SIXTEEN
JENNY

Jenny was only twelve when her Mom died. She had good friends and was pretty outgoing. I know after Jenny's mom passed away there was a subtle conspiracy between Jenny and her friends to hook me up with her friends' single moms. On one or two occasions one of these women invited me to dinner at one of their houses. I think Jenny did not want me to be alone or lonely. I went to dinner, but I was not ready to get into any kind of relationship. These friends' moms all seemed so different. I had no idea how to date or begin any type of relationship and I didn't want to either. Jenny was young in chronological years but not from a life experience point of view. She was wise beyond her years.

We moved a couple of years after her mom died to the east side of town; this was really tough for Jenny. She changed schools and it was difficult for a couple of days—until she got more friends! By this time Andy was attending the MSDB. I dropped Jenny off at school and every day after school she walked all the way home, all the way up that damn hill. When Jenny lost her mom she was going into puberty and it was such a difficult time for her. I knew nothing about puberty for girls—everything I knew about that could be put into a thimble and still have room left over. There were some adult women in her life who she could talk to. One thing I did learn is that the aisle at the grocery store with feminine products looked the same to me as all the cereal aisles. There were all kinds of pads—maxis and minis and wings. So the best thing I could do is give Jenny $20 and take her to the store.

I told her if she needed more money to just let me know.

I knew Jenny was growing up when boys came over to visit her. It was shocking to see some of these boys with spiked hair and tattoos and rings all over their bodies. They were spooky-looking bastards. None of those boys lasted—I told them to leave as soon as I saw them. When Adam was around I asked him to help me and he was happy to run them off. That didn't happen very often. I don't think Jenny was too thrilled that her older brother was running her friends off, but I encouraged it for just the spooky-looking ones. She went to proms and had new dresses and all the other things that she needed. I met her prom dates who were dressed up in their suits and looked good. After watching Adam and his friends and Jenny and her friends, I knew that she had some wild friends. I think they were a lot wilder than she was. Anyway I developed a theory—I call it the "swirling hormone theory." As a person goes into puberty and hormones become stronger, there's a vortex that automatically sets up inside the body; it becomes stronger and stronger through the teenage years and eventually the vortex dislodges the brain and sucks it right down to the gonads. And it stays there and finally, in time—generally after the teenage years— the vortex slows down and hopefully the brain floats back up to where it should be. Sometimes it never does.

Hmmm, the swirling hormone theory . . . makes sense!

Jenny worked as soon as she could. She saved her money and as soon as she was old enough she bought herself a car. She paid for everything. She paid for the car and the insurance. She was bound and determined to become as independent as possible.

I married a woman named Michelle around three years after Carla passed away. Jenny was fifteen years old at that time. The marriage only lasted for about a year and a half. So Jenny had another woman in the house that she had to deal with. This was difficult for Jenny— I believe that was a really strong motivation for Jenny to be as independent as possible and get the hell outta there. Michelle and I had a very difficult relationship. She was younger than me and did not have any children. She wanted to have fun and party, but that was basically impossible for me because I was responsible for three teenagers. It was asking a lot of her to take on three children who were nearly grown and had their own minds and did not think of her as a mother figure. I really tried to make it work; I even went into marriage counseling but Michelle refused to go. All this was going on when Jenny was only fifteen years old and still adjusting to her Mom being gone. This was not a good situation for any of us. As I said earlier Jenny was concentrating on how to grow up as fast as she could and get out of the house. Also, as Jenny was growing up she shared with me that she tried to not give me too much grief when she was young because she felt that I had suffered enough.

Right after Carla died Jenny met Bobby, her future husband, but his family soon moved to Seattle. She was twelve years old and both of them were in the seventh grade. She invited Bobby over to the house when I was at work and broke one of the rules—no boys in the house when I'm not home!

Sounds familiar!

So I read Bobby's parents, Tammy and Roger, the riot act. I think I scared Roger when I called him. I was very upset and stern regarding Bobby being over at my house. I was so mad that I said something like, "I don't know what Jenny sees in that boy." I think it really hurt Roger's feelings, and of course, Bobby was only twelve years old. As the whole family can see, Bobby has grown into a great husband and father. When Bobby's daughter is twelve he will probably understand where my concerns were coming from.

As soon as Jenny graduated from high school she moved into her own place, one of my apartments. She became very independent and lived on her own; sometimes her friends were her roommates. She worked for the Jackson Law Firm and that's where she became familiar with the law profession. Jenny really enjoyed working for the firm and she learned a great deal.

As it turned out Jenny's connection to Bobby was really powerful. After she was on her own for a while, Bobby came back into her life. They reconnected and at that time he was a single dad with a three-year-old son, Cody. They started their life together at that point and they have been together since. Cody has grown up to be a wonderful young man; Bobby and Jenny raised him together and now he is twenty-one years old. Jenny has been a wonderful mother for Cody and little Carla.

Jenny has always been such a sweet, thoughtful, and caring person. She is a survivor— very strong-willed. You certainly have been blessed to have her as your daughter. You two have really been there for each other throughout the years.

CHAPTER SEVENTEEN
AMAZING BABY CARLA

I was really concerned about how Jenny would handle stress as she approached the age that her mother was when she passed. Carla passed when she was thirty-seven years old and now Jenny is thirty-eight years old. She has now outlived her mother. This really weighed on me and now I am relieved to see that Jenny is healthy. Whatever stresses that Jenny's mom experienced during her lifetime seem like just a "drop in the bucket" compared to what Jenny has had to deal with. I always thought that stress may have had something to do with Carla's cancer. However, Jenny's stress has been really indescribable. And the worse part of it is that it has been unrelenting since baby Carla was born. Baby Carla was born with hypoplastic left heart syndrome, a very rare congenital birth defect. Jenny and Bobby, along with doctors and numerous specialists, decided to try a series of corrective heart surgeries to save her life. Baby Carla had her first three surgeries at Primary Children's Hospital in Salt Lake City, Utah. The doctors "replumbed" her heart, changing it from a four-chambered to a two-chambered heart. The left-side chambers were there; however, they were extremely underdeveloped. Carla developed extremely severe complications.

One of these complications included plastic bronchitis, which eventually was one of the major factors that required her to be placed on the heart transplant list. Carla had her heart transplant surgery in November 2012 at Seattle Children's Hospital. She was on the heart transplant waiting list for one year. Jenny and Bobby were living in

Seattle just several blocks from Children's Hospital. It has been almost three years since the transplant, and she celebrates her heartiversary every November.

Carla is our little miracle baby.

Yes, Jenny has gone through surgery after surgery with Carla—four of them since her baby was born. It was because of this unrelenting stress that I was concerned how Jenny's health would hold up over the long run. Because I know that stress has been very hard on both her and Bobby.

But with Carla's new heart, for the first time in her life, they have a chance for not having to worry about Carla's very survival at all times. Finally, after all of these years—Carla is eight years old now—there is an opportunity for some kind of normal life for their family—if you can call giving fifteen to twenty medications a day to a child normal. These are my own thoughts and feelings as I can't speak for Jenny and Bobby. Many times in her blog Jenny has expressed her own feelings. Now we all have hope and the future looks bright for Carla because of her new heart. I remember when I got to pull Carla's first loose tooth; she let me use dental floss. There is a sure sign of hope! At this time Carla has grown over thirteen inches with her new heart.

I remember one funny story when I was talking to Carla just before one of her heart catheterizations. When I asked her what she does to be brave she said, "Don't poop your pants!" I joke around with Carla now and frequently ask her how she can be so brave. I tell her, "I couldn't be so brave, I would poop my pants!" When I ask her that question about bravery, she always says to me, "Well, the first thing is don't poop your pants!"

Since the transplant Carla has had many colds and infections due to the fact that she is on immunosuppressants to prevent organ rejection. I'm afraid that this is going to be an ongoing saga. Despite all of the trials and tribulations in her life, though, it hasn't affected her spirit or her sweet personality.

Carla is so strong and such a fighter. In all my years of pediatric nursing I have fortunately seen many miracles involving children and their healing but

I feel that Carla is the biggest and most wonderful miracle I have ever witnessed.

Les (Grandpa's) song to little Carla.
"Holy Now"
By singer-songwriter Peter Mayer

When I was a boy, each week
On Sunday, we would go to church
And pay attention to the priest
He would read the holy word
And consecrate the holy bread
and everyone would kneel and bow
Today the only difference is
Everything is holy now
Everything, everything
Everything is holy now

When I was in Sunday school
We would learn about the time
Moses split the sea in two
Jesus made the water wine
And I remember feeling sad
That miracles don't happen still
But now I can't keep track
'Cause everything's a miracle
Everything, everything
Everything's a miracle

Wine from water is not so small
But an even better magic trick
Is that anything is here at all
So the challenging thing becomes
Not to look for miracles
But finding where there isn't one
When holy water was rare at best

It barely wet my fingertips
But now I have to hold my breath
Like I'm swimming in a sea of it
It used to be a world half there
Heaven's second rate hand-me-down
But I walk it with a reverent air
"Cause everything is holy now
Everything, everything
Everything is holy now

Read a questioning child's face
And say it's not a testament
That'd be very hard to say
See another new morning come
And say it's not a sacrament
I tell you that it can't be done

This morning, outside I stood
And saw a little red-winged bird
Shining like a burning bush
Singing like a scripture verse
It made me want to bow my head
I remember when church let out
How things have changed since then
Everything is holy now
It used to be a world half-there
Heaven's second rate hand-me-down
But I walk it with a reverent air
'Cause everything is holy now

CHAPTER EIGHTEEN
THE BLESSING

"We can hang on to our personal power and even grow it by forgiveness, kindness and letting go of personal judgments. Love in my life has been very pragmatic, whatever love I give to my family I get back ten-fold. It's even better than compounded interest. That doesn't mean that you have to accept being hurt but if you can find it in your heart to forgive people that have hurt you or done you wrong it is so freeing and it allows you to move on. It's a lifelong challenge to do this. I think as people get older it is easier to do this. As we get older we have a better sense of our own mortality and how precious life really is."

Author unknown; from a plaque that belongs to Sue and hangs in Les' and her home.

Sue and I met April 29, 1994. I had known about her for about a year before I ever laid eyes on her. She took her old, used, beater car to my friend David's automotive shop to have it repaired. He did all he could do to keep it running. David kept mentioning this gal to me and said he wanted to introduce her to me because she kept baking him cookies every time she brought her car in for repairs. He had introduced me to my second wife and it didn't turn out so great, so I did not want to take him up on his offer.

I did know a lot about her, though, through David. She was Catholic, went to church every Sunday, and was divorced. I kept refusing to meet her. I think after around nine months David invited Andy and me to his house and at the same time he also invited

Sue to come over. He kept trying to get Sue and I together and he finally did! I will always be grateful to him for doing that. Of course, Sue knew about me and what I had been through. One of the first things she told me is that she had been through thyroid cancer; she showed me the scar on her neck and my heart sank. When I heard the word cancer it spooked me. I didn't know where she was with her cancer, if she still had it, or if she was in remission. Sue explained to me that Dr. Crichton, a doctor she worked with in Helena at Blue Cross, noticed she had an Adam's apple on her neck and he told her to have it checked out and she did. She was diagnosed with thyroid cancer in 1993, one year before I met her. Sue had lived in Helena for about two years when we met. Prior to moving to Helena she was working for Blue Cross in Great Falls, Montana. Blue Cross asked her to transfer to the Helena office.

Sue had thyroid cancer but it was encapsulated or surrounded by normal cells so surgeons were able to remove the entire encapsulated cancer. So she did not need any type of chemotherapy or radiation. She was put on Synthroid after the surgery. Every year for five years and then, after that, once every five years until she reached ten years in remission she had to take a huge pill that contained radioactive isotope and have a full-body CT scan. The pill was given to her in a lead box and the nurse who gave it to her was completely covered. After taking the pill she couldn't be around children or pregnant women for a few days or so. She had to eat on paper plates and plastic utensils that she had to throw away after using. The worst part of the whole thing is that they had to take her off her thyroid medication for two to three weeks before having this test. Being depleted of thyroid hormone for such a long period really negatively affected her metabolism and her mood. She cried all the time. She was physically and mentally devastated one time; it was really tough on her. I think the doctors just forgot about her. I think she only needed to be off the thyroid medication for one week not three. So when she was getting really sick from the lack of her thyroid meds, sometimes I got after her to call the docs. I couldn't say too much at this time because this was before we got married. After ten years the docs declared her cancer-free.

It wasn't long after we met that I started to call her on the phone and she invited me to her house for dinner. I took my guitar and sang for my supper—mostly so I didn't have to do dishes. It wasn't long before we became pretty close. She had gotten a divorce in 1989, just about a year after Carla had died. We kind of came from similar backgrounds in terms of previous relationships. I had a wife who died and a spouse that I was divorced from. She and her ex-husband were married about the same time that Carla and I got married. She was married around eighteen years and Carla and I were married seventeen years.

I was attracted to Sue because of her independence and autonomy. Sue did not need me for anything. She was completely independent and could take care of herself and her family. She had worked for Blue Cross-Blue Shield, doing preauthorizations for organ transplant patients, longer than I had worked at my job. Also, I noticed that Sue was a really great mom; she talked to her children, Christie and Bill, every day. Christie has two lovely children, a daughter, Destiny, who is in the U.S. Navy, and a son, Tyler.

We had been dating for about a year and a half and I just knew that I would be with Sue for the rest of my life. I brought up the subject of getting married, but not directly; I was more subtle. I didn't propose, but somehow I asked her how she felt about marriage. She told me that she had no feelings about marriage at that time—none. Sue would probably dispute how the conversation evolved, but once I discerned that she wasn't interested in getting married I dropped the subject and didn't bring it up again. We continued to see each other and went on trips together. I took her to Denver to see football games when Norm was living there. We went to Las Vegas before Norm and Donna lived there. On Valentine's Day we went to the Bellagio resort and the Venetian resort, where we took a gondola ride!

There was an incident at Sue's house that happened when we were dating. One February the weather got unseasonably warm and it started raining really hard for a couple of days. Because the ground was frozen solid, serious flooding in the Helena Valley started to occur. Sue's house was in the middle of the flood; water rose right up to her door but didn't come into her house. Well, I had to rescue her. She grabbed a suitcase full of stuff and I brought her to my house. She was at my house for about three days. For three days and nights I prayed for rain and it worked! She was flooded out of her house and it took three days for the waters to subside but I kept praying for rain.

We also took a trip to Fort Jackson, an Army base in Columbia, South Carolina, to see Sue's son, Bill, graduate from boot camp in 1998. Fort Jackson graduated 4,200 people every Thursday. The base itself has about 50,000 troops. To go there we drove down to Denver and then we flew to South Carolina. We were having a lot of fun in Helena and also traveling. Anyway, we flew back on a plane and were cruising at an altitude of 33,000 feet in a big 767 and I was looking out of the window. I was concentrating on the orientation of the crops that I could see below. I tried to figure out the bearing of the plane—if we were flying northwesterly or exactly what direction we were flying. I was really concentrating. I was involved with engineering and surveying and plats for my job; I had worked with them for decades, so thinking about these things wasn't way out in left field. Surveying is all about bearings and distances. Anyway, that's what I was thinking about when all of a sudden I hear Sue's voice talking to the back of my head, "You never are going to marry me, are you?" This completely disrupted my train of thought and really surprised me. Sue, unlike me in my left-handed approach of trying to figure out if she was thinking about marriage, was much more direct—similar to that of a freight train.

But that's the sign I was looking for, so when we landed in Denver we got in our car and I drove a direct beeline to the nearest jewelry store. I'm sure I asked Norm and Donna where to go. We went to Ben Bridges and we bought rings. She found a ring she really liked, gold with diamonds. I picked out a plain gold band. When we were driving back home from Denver I noticed that she didn't have her ring on. So I asked her, "How come you're not wearing your ring?"

To which she promptly replied, "Because you haven't asked me yet." So when we got home I made it a point to formally ask her to marry me. We were at her house and she said, "Yes."

Sue and I had to go through Pre-cana classes with Father Dan Shea. He was born and raised in Anaconda, Montana, speaks eight languages, and has traveled all over the world many times. He is a sweetheart of a guy. We had to fill out many, many forms for the classes, discussing our likes and dislikes. Father Shea came to our house for these classes and we always had dinner together. I think we attended six to eight classes that were given over a period of about six months. We sat around the table and went through the classes together. As I recall, there was only one bone of contention out of perhaps nine or ten pages we had to fill out. There was one area that he saw as a potential problem and that had to do with finances, shocking both of us. We had talked about finances and knew what we had; Sue was very financially independent and did not need me for anything. So it turned out that it was just an interpretation on Father Shea's part. Sue felt $8,000 to $10,000 was a big deal where I thought $100,000 or so was a big deal. She was very frugal and careful with her money. So there was the conflict.

At that time I was juggling all kinds of property, I was dealing with my place, Mom's place, the house and land in the valley, and the McClellen place. My perspective about monetary work was on a different scale than Sue's. So Father Shea was concerned that I may have been a big spender but I never really had cash; I always had to pay a lot of expenses: property tax, insurance, maintenance costs, and automobile insurance and licenses. My property taxes and insurance were around $600 a month; of course, it is a lot more now. So I was property rich but cash poor. So $5,000 doesn't scare me if I needed it for something. As a single mom Sue had to really watch her money. Sue and I figured that this possible bone of contention helped Father Shea get a few more dinners out of us. He even said, "I think I can get a couple more dinners out of this so we can fully discuss it!"

We were married at Our Lady of the Valley Catholic Church on August 22, 1998. Sue wanted me to play an Eagle's song at our wedding so we chose "Love Will Keep Us Alive." It was good that I had about eight or nine months to learn this song. I learned it in every key because the key it was written in was way too high for my voice range. The Catholic Church doesn't even allow anything nontraditional for weddings anymore. We held our reception in the new garage at my house. Soon after I proposed I finished my basement; I remodeled it from a two-car tuck-under garage to a family room. At the same time I had the detached garage built. It was not completed by the wedding; there were no doors yet, but the roof was on. We had a fabulous time, it was 80 degrees F and blue skies.

Sue just showed me a cake that she is making for God's Love, a homeless shelter; it is called an Apple Slab cake—and it's made on a cookie sheet. She'll take it down to God's Love for their 4:00 P.M. dinner tonight. Soon she will take three dozen cupcakes down there for dinner as well.

Oh my goodness, Sue is such a blessing for God's Love.

Sue also helps at funerals at the church, and she also helps with meals once a month for God's Love. She volunteers at St. Peter's Hospital twice a week; one day she works in the gift shop and a different day she volunteers in the Alzheimer's Unit. She's the only volunteer that I know of in the Alzheimer's Unit. The hospital has a transitional unit before people are found places to live with permanent assistance. Sue became acquainted with Alzheimer's because her dad had it and he lived in a memory unit for the last two years of his life. Sue had just retired from Blue Cross-Blue Shield, so she was able to spend a lot of time in Great Falls with her folks. She sure was grateful to be retired and to be able to spend more time with her parents.

I can tell you one story about her dad, Bill, which is indicative of Alzheimer's. Bill's favorite song was "Sentimental Journey" and the first time he had heard that song was when he was coming back from WWII sailing on a ship into San Francisco Bay. He was actually in the Army but was stationed on a boat transporting Australian solders to little islands in the Pacific to fight the Japanese. Knowing about his favorite song, I bought a book of standards from the '30s and '40s to learn how to play it on my guitar. When I played "Sentimental Journey" for him he was so emotional that tears came to his eyes. As he was becoming very sick with Alzheimer's he needed to be placed in a memory unit. When Sue and I visited him I brought my guitar and played "Sentimental Journey" for him and then I played another song. Then Bill said, "You know my favorite song is 'Sentimental Journey,' do you know that song?" So I played it again. I usually played his favorite song for him eight to ten times during my visits with him. Toward the end of Bill's life, when his Alzheimer's was quite severe, I played "Sentimental Journey" for him and I asked him if he recognized the song and he said no. It wasn't too long after Bill forgot his favorite song that he passed from this life and went to heaven. Sue's mom, Agnes, insisted on living with Bill at the memory unit. This was tough for Agnes because she was the only one with a sound mind who lived there. It really broke Agnes' heart to see her husband deteriorate and at the end, not remember who she was. Sue's favorite saint is Saint Agnes. Sue and her brothers, especially her brother Bruce, took exemplary care of their parents as they became older and needed more help.

It was so hard on Sue when she lost her mom. They were so close. They talked on the phone every day. Sue is so much like her mom—they were so similar. Her mom taught Sue all of her homemaking skills; she learned how to cook and sew from her mom. The way she reacts to her children and grandchildren, she learned all of that from her mom. All of the good qualities that Sue has that you look for in a spouse and friend, Sue has; they are a reflection of her mother and her upbringing. This reminds me of Jenny and how much she is like her mom.

I've known Sue and have been with her longer than I was with Carla. Not that that means anything; it's just that life goes on. I feel really fortunate and blessed that I was given a second chance at happiness. The second time around you have a deeper appreciation of the blessings that you've been given. When a person is young he or she just doesn't know what they have; after they lose it only then will they understand what they really had in their life. As I have gotten older

I really know what I have in my life and really appreciate it. Sue and I have so many friends who are widowed or divorced and so we realize that we are so fortunate to have found each other and have the life we have at this time. It's impossible to take our life together for granted after what we have been through. We both feel the same way about this. Our kids also feel that we are so blessed to have found each other. At this time in our life we are both retired, we have some financial security, and we have our health. We really can't ask for more. I think life for me is best when shared with someone who I love. There are all kinds of circumstances that set the stage for being alone. Relationships can be devastating and for some people life is just easier without them. Relationships are not for all people. But for me I know that my life is more fulfilling with Sue in it. It's wonderful to be able to share life with someone who loves you.

Life is a gift; none of us asked to be born, but we were. There are a lot of things out of our control, but there are some things that are in our control and I think it takes a lifetime of living to realize what is important and what is not. Over a lifetime a person loses all kinds of people who are close to them, usually starting with a parent but sometimes a spouse or child, but these losses make you see your own mortality. I'm grateful for the life that I've been given. I experienced some very serious or bad things in my life, but if I weighed the good against the bad, the scale of my life is heavy toward the good. The reality is my life would be incalculably more toward the good than anything else. I think it's important to not let the bad things that happen determine the outcome of your life. The purpose that these bad things can serve is to make a person appreciate the good in life so much more.

A friend is one to whom one may pour out all the contents of one's heart, chaff and grain together, knowing that the gentlest of hands will take and sift it, keep what is worth keeping and, with a breath of kindness blow the rest away.

Arabian Proverb, from a plaque that hangs in Les and Sue's home.

"Lucky One"
by Amy Grant and Keith Thomas 1994
For Les and Sue

You're the kind
When you love, you love with all your
Might and
You're the kind
I would dream about at night
Now I'm the lucky one
Baby I'm the lucky one

You're the kind
That I want to be with in the dark and
You're the kind
Who is capturing my heart
And I'm the lucky one
Baby I'm the lucky one

And I have never been the one to fall in
Love so soon
But I could never face another night or day
Without you,
Baby I'm the lucky one

You're the kind with poetry and Valentines and
You're the kind
Who will never ever leave and I'm the
Lucky one
The luckiest girl, my, my, my baby
Baby I'm the lucky one

And I have never been the one to fall in
Love so soon
But I could never face another night or day
Without you, you, I'm the lucky one
Baby I'm the lucky one

And I have never been the one to fall in
Love so soon
But I could never face another night or day
Without you, you, I'm the lucky one

CHAPTER NINETEEN

FINAL THOUGHTS

Baby I'm the lucky one

So you're retired now. I'm glad, you deserve it! Any thoughts about retirement?

It's good! Every day is Saturday! This is why I worked my whole dang life—for security and happiness. I just feel really blessed in my life. Life is best shared and I was given another opportunity—to share my life with Sue—that's about as good as it gets.

My Sister
By Les Morgan, 1969

My sister, Jeannette, is the only person I feel that I know well enough to write about. I have other brothers and sisters, but Jeannette I feel I know better than anyone else.

She is five feet, four inches tall and weighs about one hundred and fifteen pounds. This last fact, of course, is only a guess since she would never let a secret like that go. She has soft, fine light brown hair; large, sparkling blue eyes; and a light pink complexion. Her hands seem delicate but her fingers and wrists are strong from playing the piano for the past seven years.

It used to be a few years ago, when she had the figure of a broomstick, that she would get twenty phone calls a night from girls alone. Now, since her figure has changed considerably, she still receives the twenty calls from girls, but she also gets ten or fifteen from boys.

One of her hobbies, besides boys, is writing to pen pals. She writes to people in Switzerland, Italy, and Vietnam. It seems as though she's either getting or sending a letter every day.

One of her hobbies is sleeping in on school days. You can imagine what she is like on days like this. If it isn't too late, she'll come ambling out of her room, groggy eyed and hair put up in rollers. If it is too late, she'll come storming out like she had just discovered a bear in her bed, arms flailing, and squawking like a chicken with its head cut off.

In the final view my sister is a very fine person. She is very sensitive and feels for other people and their problems. I would, for this reason, never trade my sister for any other.

"Grateful"
By Jeannette Morgan Yim, January 2015

I'm grateful I grew up with you,
both July babies two years apart.

Your goofy sense of humor helped ease
the unpredictable struggles that we faced.

You were stable, I could count on you.
You were always the same,
your character did not change.

In our crazy, chaotic, and at times
violent childhood, you were a rock.
I never saw you get swallowed
by erupting volcanoes.

You were sanity. Your Gibson and sweet voice
were beautiful.

They brought me peace.
I'm grateful I grew up with you,
both July babies two years apart.

BIOGRAPHY

Jeannette Morgan Yim was raised in Helena, Montana. She and her husband, Bill, enjoy their three grown children and six grandchildren.

She attended both private Catholic school and public schools. She graduated from Helena High School in 1972 and received a BA in nursing from Carroll College in Helena. She later attended California State University, Sacramento, where she received a Masters of Science in nursing. The majority of her nursing career has been in pediatrics in the hospital and in public health settings in Sacramento, California, because of her love for children.

As a recent retiree, Jeannette continues to pursue her love of music and piano. She also loves gardening, traveling, and dancing. One of her favorite pastimes is spending quality time with her grandchildren.

Les Morgan was raised in Helena, Montana. He attended both private Catholic schools and public school. He graduated from Helena High School in 1969 and received a BA degree in biology from Carroll College in Helena in 1973.

The majority of Les' career has been working in the engineering field from 1969 through 2014 when he retired from the City of Helena Engineering Department.

His major interests include music and playing the guitar, which he has played in a band for many years.

He enjoys spending time with his three grown children, daughter-in-law and son-in-law, and two stepchildren with their families, including six grandchildren. He enjoys quality time with his family, and traveling with his wife, Sue.

Les also spends a great deal of time taking care of his elderly mother with the help of his wife and sister.